Praise for the Author

"My opportunity to work with Steve Welling was pleasant and positive. I would work with him anytime. I know this book will be helpful."

— **DR. JOHN K. JENKINS SR.**, Senior Pastor First Baptist Church of Glenarden and President of Converge

"Steve Welling calls out the best in people. He invites leaders to engage their highest calling and rally those they lead to join them on the mission. Steve's coaching enabled me to maximize the impact of our leadership teams, releasing the creative energy of untapped members of the group. Steve's impact can still be measured three years after his consultation with our leadership team."

— **DR. WES JOHNSON**, ThM, DMin, retired pastor, Bethel Baptist Church, Everett WA

"Steve Welling uses his decades of business management and consulting experience from both the commercial and the religious non-profit fields to distill the five basic concepts that any goal seeker needs to know to achieve success and communicates those with love and humor!"

> — **MARK HAYNES**, Mark Haynes Productions CEO and Executive Producer

"Serving with Steve was always a delight, from the first conversation to the results. Steve models and genuinely exhibits three great qualities of a team member and ministry partner. He listens intently, thinks inquisitively, and responds intuitively with selfless motives and concern for others. While listening, Steve asked questions to be sure that we were on the same page and moving in the same direction. After affirming a course for action, it was clear how he carefully thought through the issue, process and outcomes. His clarity in thinking and articulating our united pursuit led to selfless engagement. This kind of response always left me and others confident to know Steve was in the process to see others grow, mature and be advantaged. I wish others could learn from Steve's open heart, mind and positive pathways. We can all learn how to lead from Steve Welling."

> — **DR. DOUG FAGERSTROM**, The CEO Forum Senior Discipleship Fellow | Member Engagement and Discipleship

"I got to know Steve during his tenure as the Regional President of Converge Northwest. In that capacity, he worked relationally with every church in the region. What a blessing when he came to my church and led us through a visioning process! The resulting vision is still bearing fruit many years later. Whether at the individual or the organizational level, get ready for a journey of transformation, led by a master coach!"

— **DR. THERESA SCHAUDIES**, Spiritual Director

"The delight in working with Steve is not only to view the process, one of definition, clarity, and vision, but to see his heart for mentoring. He is for the good, the very best for the life path of those who are the recipients of his thoughtful care."

— **MICKEY COOK**, Business Owner

"There is a lot of talking today but little listening. A lot of dialog but little meaningful conversation. Unfortunately, at times, this is true in the church as well. Steve Welling's "5 Conversations" comes at a time when society and the church are desperate for the gift of meaningful conversation. This book, along with Steve's years of ministry experience and consulting expertise, provide a foundation for ministry direction (refocus) and advancement."

— **BRUCE SUMNER**, Regional President Converge Southwest

"As a result of working with Steve, a skilled coach and mentor, I have been able to move from coping to overcoming."

— **KRISY CORLEY**, Special Needs Educator

"Thank you so much for this great opportunity to put in writing my appreciation for you and your ministry. Having the privilege of serving with you was an honor to see your humility in serving others in the attempt to bring out the best in them. Through your experiences of pain and difficulty, you have been able to mine out truths that folks can follow and apply to their lives to move forward to the completion of their mission. Your courage and tenacious spirit have shown me time and time again to keep my eyes on what is critically important and never, never give up doing the hard work of working issues to their finality. Thank you, Steve."

— **ROY PEACOCK**, Pastor Raging River Community Church

"I've known Steve for many years. As a co-laborer, his office door was always open to mentor me and develop me into the leader that he could envision me becoming. Now, I strive to do the same for others in my spheres of influence."

— **RYAN HUEBNER**, Lead Pastor - Osceola Grace Church

"I appreciate Steve's attentiveness in all of our conversations. His ability to provide clarity and perspective has encouraged me to take good next steps in my personal ministry. Steve brings a wealth of experience and lives out what he teaches."

— **TIM STOBBE**, Lead Pastor - Waypoint Church

"Steve has an amazing gift of listening between the lines and asking powerful questions to help people discern what actions are needed to move forward. His inviting demeanor, profound experience, and ability to help others understand things they didn't know about themselves, make him a trusted coach, and allows those he works with to unlock their full potential."

— **BRIAN CANFIELD,** Founder Northwest Apogee

"I appreciate Steve's ability to take abstract concepts and provide clarity and direction in order to move forward. I had the opportunity to work with Steve Welling and found that I was able to grow in my own leadership as a result of spending time with him. Steve Welling is a true friend and encourager. I appreciate his ability to help others feel empowered and find courage to step into new endeavors with confidence. The one thing I would like to say about Steve's work is that it is consistent, insightful and inspiring."

— **DAN CARLSON**, Care Pastor Wooddale Church

"Steve has an uncanny ability to recognize the untapped potential in others. More than that, he is able to ask the right questions in order to bring about self-discovery and growth. I'm a better leader today because Steve believed and invested in my development long before I had a vision of what could be."

— **DR. NATE HETTINGA**, Regional President Converge Northwest

"Steven is the mentor that any big organization needs to grow its leadership. In his book, "The Five Conversations", Steven offers a step by step blueprint to build the right leadership skills by mastering the art of conversation."

— **MUSTAFA AMMAR**, CEO & Founder of The Passion MBA

"Steve has been a mentor to me for over four decades. In every phase of our relationship, he has not only given me solid, actionable advice, but has helped me develop my own decision-making skills for when I don't have him on speed dial. Whether you are mentored by Steve in person, or by reading this book, you will get great insight into what makes Steve the gifted mentor that he is."

— **KATHI LIPP**, Author of *Clutter Free*

"The number one thing I appreciate about Steve is his ability to listen. He engages with people by asking questions, so he can learn more about them.

I had the opportunity to be mentored by Steve Welling during the pandemic lock down. He presented zoom training on leadership. I learned many valuable lessons about how to be a leader. I learned to focus on building up people as opposed to using them to reach a goal.

It is clear that one big thing about Steve is that he loves people and this drives how he goes about working to grow leaders. I know he helped me grow."

— **TED TURNER**, Computer Analyst, Goalkeeper & Church Elder

"For several decades I've experienced Steve's contagious commitment as a teacher and mentor who champions personal growth, facilitates relationship-building, and stimulates a broader vision and forward progress in those he serves and leads"

— **CATHIE VARCOE MULLINS**, Human Resources Specialist

"When others see problems, Steve sees solutions."

— **DR. TOM HARRIS**, President - Interim Pastor Ministries

"Steve has an affinity for asking engaging and thought-provoking questions that help people step forward in personal relationships, and that have been a key part of his career helping corporate and nonprofit organizations move toward their potential."

— **JIM GREETHAM**, School Teacher

"I had the opportunity to work with Steve Welling for nearly 15 years of coaching, training, and mentoring our Vietnamese Pastors and Church Leaders across the USA and globally. I have learned from Steve Welling a lot of practical tools that not only dissect change but also provide hope that the constancy of change need not be feared but relished to help any leaders to be effective for life. He explains how to anticipate leadership challenges and make them manageable.

Steve Welling is a fun and dynamic speaker with all of the truths he has experienced for himself, that make his teachings hit straight to the hearts of people.

The one thing I would like to say about Steve's work is a must-read for anyone who wants to change for the better of their personal life, family, and business."

— **REV. DR. PHU PHAM**, Converge Asia Impact Team Facilitator

"After publishing over 230 Chicken Soup for the Soul book titles and working with hundreds of authors and thousands of contributors, I have met all kinds of people. Some good, some great and some genuinely amazing. Steve Welling is one of them - genuinely amazing. The moment I met Steve, I knew he was special, and each time we get together and talk, I am reminded again and again of his authenticity and his transparency. He is simply a good human, who cares about others and serves intentionally with purpose. Whether it is one of his books, a program, a sermon, a keynote, he is consistently excellent."

— **PATTY AUBERY**, NY Times Best-selling Author, *Chicken Soup for the Christian Soul*. President, Jack Canfield Companies

"There are few who are both well balanced and clearly focused in the executive world. Steve Welling is one of them.
I had the privilege to recruit Steve for a key non-profit leadership position. I found that Steve is stellar, solid, wise, patient and calm. Yet was able to move the necessary forward in a good direction. I see why Steve was successful. It wasn't what he knows or even his talented teaching skills. It was his ability to ask the right questions. He asked open ended questions which causes one to stop in their tracks and reflect on the whole, not just the part you may want. I learned that if you can master the supreme art of asking probing questions one can bring unity out of division and joy out of despair."

— **GLENN REPH**, Serial Entreprenuer

The 5 conversations

conversations

A Mentor's Strategy for Uncommon Success

STEVEN B WELLING

Copyright © 2023, Steve B. Welling

ISBN Softcover: 979-8-88739-045-1
ISBN Ebook: 979-8-88739-046-8

Printed in the United States of America.

All rights reserved. No part of this book may be reproduced or transmitted in any form or by any means, electronic or mechanical, including photocopying, recording or by any information storage and retrieval system, without permission in writing from the copyright owner. For information on distribution rights, royalties, derivative works or licensing opportunities on behalf of this content or work, please contact the publisher at the address below.

Unless otherwise noted, scripture quotations are from:
Scriptures taken from the Holy Bible, New International Version®, NIV®. Copyright © 1973, 1978, 1984, 2011 by Biblica, Inc.™ Used by permission of Zondervan. All rights reserved worldwide. www.zondervan.com The "NIV" and "New International Version" are trademarks registered in the United States Patent and Trademark Office by Biblica, Inc.®

All Scripture quotations are taken from *The Message*, copyright © 1993, 2002, 2018 by Eugene H. Peterson. Used by permission of NavPress. All rights reserved. Represented by Tyndale House Publishers.

Although the author and publisher have made every effort to ensure that the information and advice in this book was correct and accurate at press time, the author and publisher do not assume and hereby disclaim any liability to any party for any loss, damage, or disruption caused from acting upon the information in this book or by errors or omissions, whether such errors or omissions result from negligence, accident, or any other cause.

I dedicate this book to my wife, Susie. She has been walking with me for more than 47 years, watching me grow up, grow out, and grow older. Her faithful support while I sought to find and stretch myself and take risks allowed me to discover whole new worlds of opportunity. Thank you, Susie, for believing in me.

Table of Contents

Introduction . . . . *xix*

Chapter 1: We Have Lift Off. 25
Chapter 2: I Don't Know How to Drive 33
Chapter 3: I Think We Missed Something, Part 1 45
Chapter 4: I Think We Missed Something, Part 2 57
Chapter 5: Is That You? 67
Chapter 6: Living with Vision. 81
Chapter 7: How Do They Know Where We Are Going? 97
Chapter 8: The Authenticity Conversation:
    Who Am I Now?. 117
Chapter 9: Light A Fire – Choices, Leadership
    and Legacy 133

Notes *145*
Acknowledgments *147*
About the Author *149*
About the Company. *151*

Introduction

Conversations around five questions can change your life.

This is a personal book. I tell some of my stories, but the real story is yours. I hope you can add significant depth and meaning to your life by gleaning from my attempt to share from my experiences. My desire is to serve you on your journey.

It is predicted that we are heading into some challenging years ahead. Questions about safety, financial security and personal values in the marketplace come naturally. How will you handle the challenges in the years to come? Is it a matter of being better than everyone else? Needing to be better is a tough way to live. Better than who? Better at what? It can feel like an endless chase. What I do know is that some people will be successful in the days ahead. Will you be one of them?

Maybe you wonder with me what this world needs. I think we need more joyful people, who are making life work and living life well. Sometimes I think this world needs deeper people. Then I could say my ultimate goal in life is to develop deeper people. If you are looking for a quick fix, this book isn't it; this book is the roadmap for a journey that takes time. I can't predict how long it will take an individual to travel the road. But I have learned that it can be traveled. This book is for those who want to join me in developing deeper people. I am writing this for those who want to make the world a better place, people who are growing, thought by thought, into healthy, holistically integrated humans, living joyfully on purpose. As Charles Swindoll wrote,

> Deep things are intriguing. Deep jungles. Deep water. Deep caves and canyons. Deep thoughts and conversations. There is nothing like depth to make us dissatisfied with superficial, shallow things. Once we have delved below the surface and had a taste of the marvels and mysteries of the deep, we realize the value of taking the time and going to the trouble of plumbing those depths. [1]

Deep people are worth knowing.

When I say "deep", I am not talking about deep in the sense of owning a fancy degree, stoic personality or being a guru on the mountain top. I am talking about being a person of integrity with high character and internal peace. It seems our culture is not talking about this type of personal success these days. In our culture, that kind of life is an Uncommon Success. I believe it is time to get back to talking peacefully about things that make us better people. The current trend of shouting doesn't seem to be effective in developing people of depth. I think conversations can.

Sometimes I think this world needs more noble people. They don't have to be perfect. But I would love to see a world where more people care about others. I think noble people would behave unselfishly, lifting others while living the kind of life that

INTRODUCTION

is meaningful. My life could be dedicated to developing noble people. Noble people are worth knowing.

Sometimes I think this world needs healthier leaders. Emotionally healthy leaders whose lives integrate higher principles and real-world wisdom. I call this kind of person an *attractional leader*. I would like to see these attractional leaders invest themselves in others so that there are more successful people. I would love to say my ultimate goal in life is to help develop healthy leaders. Healthy leaders are worth knowing.

It is a daunting task, but I decided to write a book that seeks to capture enough information and strategy that a person could become a deep, noble and healthy leader. In my view, becoming a person worth knowing is Uncommon Success.

To make sense of this book, here are some things to understand.

First, the title is *the 5 Conversations*. This refers to five types of conversations that need to be navigated in life. Each type of conversation will be an ongoing dialogue that varies in the amount of time needed. It could take days, weeks or months. You get to set the pace.

Since I am an ordained minister, you might expect a lot of God talk. But this is not an explicitly religious book. My faith experience seeps through a few times when I mention Bible verses or Bible characters. But those leaks are few. If you notice it at all, I will say my faith is more implied rather than proclaimed. If you are a part of the faith community and would like a "baptized" version of the material, I am writing a follow-up Faith Version Workbook.

I want this book to be for anyone interested in successfully guiding others, whether they see it as a faith journey or life journey.

Finally, this book is truly about a process of life change. I believe the process can save you from years of getting stuck, trapped or sidetracked by enemies of growth. You can become the very best version of who you are if you are willing to do the work. I believe that you can be a deep, noble, healthy person who experiences Uncommon Success! And when you do, you can mentor others to experience it too.

How to Read this Book

Whether you are a leader, emerging leader, mentor or want to learn how to be a mentor, you can gain much from this book.

The 5 Conversations are really about answering five questions in life.

1. Where am I?

2. Who am I?

3. Where am I going?

4. How am I going to get there?

5. How do I stay comfortable in my own skin when I am changing?

INTRODUCTION

There are no rules here, but the questions make sense in their order. I suggest studying the chapters in order. But if you want to jump ahead, do so. Make this journey your own.

If you are ready for the challenge, let us begin.

Rev. Steven B. Welling

We Have Lift Off

> "Being worth knowing is more important
> than being well known."
> — Anonymous

Sometimes it just takes a while to do what you think you are supposed to do.

Twenty-five years ago, I decided I needed to do something. I am getting around to it today. It usually doesn't take me that long to get something done, let alone started. But in this case, it has taken me a quarter century to gather enough courage.

Maybe you can feel my pain. At the time, I was a struggling pastor of a small congregation. I had served in bigger churches with some level of success, but this new assignment was different than what I was used to. Up until that point, I had served in and led churches with multiple staff members and hundreds of attendees each week. The new assignment was a small church that had gone through a split, and my first Sunday there, we had sixty people in attendance. I didn't know it at the time, but the small church is different. Which is a way of saying I found it to be an extremely difficult congregation for me to lead. All of my familiar patterns of leading were not effective, and the congregation was not as responsive to my leadership. I took on this flock with the idea that I would lead it into a promised land of joy, with growing attendance, and all would see my ministerial success.

While we did see mild progress (the attendance doubled in size in the first year), we didn't see the growth I felt we needed. The church's and our personal finances were always a strain. Eventually, I made the move to become bi-vocational, and I went to work for a seminar company that taught management skills around the country. I was paid a flat fee for each day that I presented an all-day seminar. But I could earn additional income by selling motivational and educational materials as well. This is where I first started learning about Stephen Covey and his *7 Habits of Highly Effective People*; Brian Tracy and the *Psychology of Success*; Jack Canfield's *Self-Esteem and Peak Performance* and other authors and speakers. While traveling each week around the country to present the seminars, I would study from these thought leaders. I began putting their principles to work in my life, and I began to experience significant change.

This is when I decided I needed to do something. I gathered my family around and made an announcement: I was planning to write a book. It was a great moment. My young daughters were wide eyed and excited for me. My wife was eager to hear more.

CHAPTER 1: WE HAVE LIFT OFF

That is when it happened. They asked me the inevitable question: "What are you going to write about?"

I said, "I am going to write a book about success."

At that moment my family burst into laughter. It wasn't the kind of timid giggle from a bad joke in church. This was spontaneous combustion. It was immediate. It took off like a rocket when the control center counted down and announces, "We have lift off." Only, in my case, it wasn't a lift off. It was a crash and burn. Like a pin into a balloon, deflation came suddenly.

I can look back to that moment and thank my family for their innocent and painful honesty. I wasn't ready to write a book about life and success. But what did get launched was my journey into applying the principles I was learning and wanted to share them with you in this book. Twenty-five years later, I have the courage to share with you what I learned when I applied principles of success.

During those twenty-five years, I finished out my time at that small church and then handed the flock off to the next pastor. He has been there ever since. I then started my own consulting business where I had the opportunity to coach executives and consult in businesses. I spoke in nearly every state in the U.S. and in the United Kingdom, and I spent thousands of hours standing in front of people presenting business seminars. I worked at this business for five years before I felt called back into ministry and served as the Senior Associate Pastor of a very large church.

I also began serving on national and regional overseer boards and became a denominational Regional President (Think Baptist Bishop) overseeing the co-operative work of over 100 churches. I led that work for more than thirteen years before I reached retirement age. In those five years of living with newly implemented principles, I moved from leading a congregation of 100 people to leading more than 100 congregations across a five-state region and held national ministry responsibilities. But more important than increased responsibilities, I moved from a sense of "just hanging on" to a feeling that "my life is working." This was a huge leap for me. Earlier, I had been standing up on Sunday mornings and telling people how life worked. But the truth was, personally, my life was not working.

It was a journey to get there, but I found it to be worth the effort.

What Is Success?

I call this new position where life is working "Uncommon Success." It is the understanding, with conviction, that who you are is far more important than others' opinions. That is another way of saying that being worth knowing is more important than being well known. It is Uncommon Success in some ways because it contrasts with the most common beliefs about success as seen in a dictionary definition.

Success – adjective. achieving or *having achieved success. having attained wealth, position, honors*, or the like (italics, mine).

Success as a topic is very popular, but getting hold of it is like chasing a greased pig. When you do the research, there seems to be no end to the possible ways to define success in creative ways. Mark Twain sarcastically wrote, "All you need in this life is ignorance and confidence, and then success is sure."

Some of my favorite mentors have offered more helpful descriptions of success.

Zig Ziglar: "Success means doing the best we can with what we have. Success is the doing, not the getting; in the trying, not the triumph. Success is a personal standard, reaching for the

CHAPTER 1: WE HAVE LIFT OFF

highest that is in us, becoming all that we can be. Success is about achieving the best version of yourself."

Jim Rohn: "Success is doing ordinary things, extraordinarily well."

Brian Tracy: "Success is the ability to live your life the way you want to live it, doing what you most enjoy, surrounded by people who you admire and respect."

John Maxwell: "Success is ... knowing your purpose in life, growing to reach your maximum potential, and sowing seeds that benefit others."

Jack Canfield: "Success is the fulfillment of your soul's purpose."

I like each of those definitions.

What you learn from these quotes is that success is far more than a version of, "He who dies with the most toys wins." Success is not just about acquisition. It is far more nuanced. When I talk about Uncommon Success, I am saying being worth knowing is of more importance than being well known. Knowing where you are, who you are, where you are going, having a plan to get there and managing yourself through the transitions that invariably need to take place when you arrive. It is not so much a destination as it is knowing how to find personal satisfaction on the journey. *Uncommon Success is joyfully living on purpose as you become more of who you were always meant to be.* I will say it again, being worth knowing is of more importance than being well known. That is Uncommon Success.

The Journey Ahead

I have spent a few years as a road warrior. I was one of those people who travels a lot to go to meetings and spends too much time in airports. On one particular trip, I was reading *Undaunted Courage*, about the Lewis and Clark expedition. I was struck by the fact that it took them 18 months to reach the Pacific Ocean from St. Louis. I wasn't struck by their need for 18 months of travel; I was struck by the fact that I was covering the same distance in three hours.

You may be asking whether you can joyfully live on purpose and become more the person you want to be. Can you get there? Can you too experience Uncommon Success? The answer is a bold "Yes!" But it is a yes with some conditions.

First, recognize that this will be a journey. It does not happen in a matter of hours. There are no jets to help you cover the distance faster. This journey will take time. Like Lewis and Clark, you will find surprises along the way. Journeys always have twists, turns and surprises. You will benefit from having a guide or mentor.

Next, you need to understand that, as you follow this path, you will experience change. Most likely it will be a deep change. I like how Robert E Quinn explains deep change in his book *Deep Change*:

> Deep change differs from incremental change in that it requires new ways of thinking and behaving. Changes that are major in scope are discontinuous with the past and generally irreversible. Deep change efforts distort existing patterns of action and involve taking risks. [2]

Finally, I want to point out that, on this journey, there are enemies that cause you to get stuck. When you feel stuck, you may be in one of their traps. These enemies and traps are common. I find some people get comfortable living a stuck life. As

CHAPTER 1: WE HAVE LIFT OFF

you continue to read, I will point out some of these common enemies. You will meet Almost True Stu, Bumper Car Karl and a few others who have fallen victim or enjoyed creating victims.

You may wonder why I am so confident that this journey can be made successfully. I have discovered that the journey toward Uncommon Success is most commonly approached in a haphazard way. While some may not want to take the risk, there are others with higher aspirations. They may hope to get there but are not strategic about the process of change.

I come to you as one who has traveled this path. Someone else's laughter no longer deflates me. I have helped guide others along the journey.

You will discover that this is a strategic path. It will take more than a few hours, but it doesn't have to take you a lifetime when you have a strategic mentor who can guide you in the right conversations, as found in this book. The conversations are in strategic order. Each is important to provide a foundation for the next conversation.

My greatest hope is that those who take on this journey to Uncommon Success will discover a deeply satisfying life. One of joy and purpose. A life of comfort in their own skin and becoming the best version of themselves. Then take what is learned and become a mentor to others.

You can experience this deep life change and mentor others on this path through two key skills. The next chapter covers those skills of mentoring and strategic conversations.

I have lifted off. Are you ready to lift off too?

Questions for Reflection

1. Are you where you want to be in life?

2. What is your definition of success?

3. Who do you know who could use help in finding Uncommon Success?

I Don't Know How to Drive

"Have you ever been scared but you
knew you had to do it anyway?"
— Anonymous

After taking the bus across town in June of 1969 to start my drivers ed. program, I walked nervously into Lewis and Clark High School. At age fifteen, I had just completed my freshman year of high school at a junior high. This was "big time" because I was walking into a real high school and was going to learn how to drive.

When I went into the classroom, much to my dismay, my 9th grade Spanish teacher, Mr. Kerley, was standing in front. I think he was as disheartened as I was when our eyes connected. He probably had seen my name on his class list, but it wasn't real until I walked through the door. My presence didn't make him smile. I had not been a "supremo" student in his class. I was usually going for the easy joke instead of the hard work of learning a new language. However, we joined again, and we each made the best of it.

I have one crystal-clear memory from our time together that summer. It came the day when I finally had the opportunity to get behind the wheel and drive the car. I had been sitting in the backseat while two other students took their turn to drive. We were on the north side of town when my turn came, and it was time to head back to the south side. All went well. I was confident on the straight, flat road. I was good with ninety-degree turns. Left, right, no problem.

As we headed south on N. Ash Street, we went to a downhill section that first curved left, then back to right, before it curved left again to straighten out. We were halfway down that hill, and the car was speeding up on its own. Something to do with gravity. I felt out of control. The car was out of control. I had a moment of panic, let go of the steering wheel, and I shouted out, "I don't know how to drive." The boys in the back were in their own panic, preparing for the impact.

Mr. Kerley calmly pressed the brake pedal that was installed on his passenger side and said, "Grab the wheel. You can do this."

I did as I was told. We made it down the hill without crashing. Our hearts returned to their normal pace, and Mr. Kerley remained calm. He was right ... I could do it. I broke through a barrier that day and learned that I could control the car and not let the car control me. Mr. Kerley and I got along very well after that, and I passed drivers ed.

It wasn't until much later that I realized I had broken through a personal barrier. I felt the fear but with help, did what I needed to do. At sixteen, I passed my driver's test and got my license, but at age fifteen was I when I learned to drive, when he said, "You can do this." And I did.

As you read this book and explore the mentoring challenge, it may sound a little scary to believe that you can guide another person into a life of Uncommon Success. You may feel like your own life has a few curves in it. Maybe you feel like your life has been going downhill lately. Maybe you have been tempted to just take your hands off the wheel and say, "I can't do this." I want to be the calm voice next to you saying, "You can do this."

Let me slow you down and let you know you can feel the fear and do it anyway. I say this with confidence. You do not need special talents to be a guide on the journey. But, like me, with learning how to drive a car, it is important to learn a couple of key skills. Skills, by definition, are things you can learn. Developing more skills simply makes you a more valuable person. As Jim Rohn says, "Don't wish it was easier, wish you were better. Don't wish for less problems, wish for more skills."

For our purposes, we will look at two skills needed to become a strategic mentor. They are learning how to mentor and how to have a productive conversation. If you are willing to do those two things, you can guide another person through the journey to Uncommon Success.

The Skill of Mentoring

What is meant by the skill of mentoring? In the current ecosystem of people development, there are a variety of terms that get used. You will hear counselor, coach (of all kinds), teacher, trainer, educator and tutor. I have chosen to use the term "mentor" for specific reasons. The word comes from Homer's book *The Odyssey*. Mentōr was the name of the advisor of the young Telemachus.

When you look for a technical definition of a mentor, you discover that it essentially means a "wise advisor."

I prefer the term mentor because it implies an intentional relationship. The mentor is a person willing to take time for the mentee. This person is available for the long haul and to build a trusting relationship. A mentor is a person who takes the time to listen deeply and provide guidance from their own experience and what they have learned. As a relationship-based model, the opportunity is there to work over an extended time and help the mentee navigate *the 5 Conversations* journey through deep change.

There is a cost to this kind of investment in strategically mentoring another person. Explaining the cost reminds me of how I coached my kids through college. I would say to them that there are four secrets to successfully getting through college:

- Show Up. In college, it was show up for class. As a mentor, show up emotionally. A good mentor is one who cares about the mentee.
- Read Up. In college, the challenge was to stay ahead of the reading demands of a class. It was hard to catch up if you fell behind. As a mentor, you keep learning

about personal and professional development. This will be helpful to your mentee. You will be modeling life-long learning.
- Keep Up. In college, you had to turn your assignments in on time. As a mentor, you keep the relationship fresh by making consistent time for your mentee. You will model reliability and integrity.
- Finish Well. In college, you push through to the end of the class. The mentor pushes through tough times with the mentee to complete the process. This will be a challenging journey. Your mentee will need your support as they experience the growth pains of breaking barriers. Working through strategic conversations is not a sprint. It's closer to a marathon. Like a marathon runner, determine the right pace to finish. There will be times when you will want to slow down. That is appropriate. But keep moving in the right direction even when it feels like a long walk.

You will enjoy practicing your mentoring skills. One of the reasons is that you will be practicing conversation skills.

The Skill of Conversation

A few years ago, I met up with a friend whom I hadn't seen for years. We started talking, and the next thing I knew, four hours had gone by. That was a fun conversation. That is what we are looking for as a strategic mentor. We don't need to have four-hour encounters, but we want to have conversations that are informative, interesting, challenging and ultimately transformational. Conversation is the natural way we come together.

Leadership author and consultant, Margaret Wheatley, transformed my thinking about the value of conversations twenty years ago. I read *Turning To One Another*, which is subtitled, *simple conversations to restore hope to the future*. In the book, she lays out the importance and power of simple conversations. I'll give you just a little taste.

> Whenever I read about a new humanitarian relief effort – some of which have earned the Nobel Peace Prize – it is always a story of the power of conversation. Somewhere in the description of how it all began is the phrase: 'Some friends and I started talking…'
> It is always like this. Real change begins with the simple act of people talking about what they care about.
>
> I can't think of anything that's given me more hope recently than to observe how simple conversations that originate deep in our caring give birth to powerful actions that change lives and restore hope to the future.
>
> It takes courage to start a conversation. But if we don't start talking to one another, nothing will change. Conversation is the way we discover how to transform our world together.[3]

This thinking is what challenged me to consider how to use mentoring conversations to help people grow. Conversation is the primary way people grow. Why not step into mentoring with a strategy of focused conversations? Through conversation we process our story. We clarify who we are. We articulate our beliefs and plans of action. It is through conversation that we review, revive, refine, refocus, re-purpose and re-invent. Conversation leads to shifts in thinking. Change your thinking and you change your life. There is great power in conversation. There is even more power in a great conversation. Strategic mentoring is all about using conversation for a purpose and a plan. We talk about how to joyfully live on purpose. We talk about becoming more of who we were always meant to be.

To have a conversation is not difficult. To be skilled in conversation takes effort. Like any skill, you can practice. You can improve. You can do this.

Good Conversation Ingredients

There are three fundamental ingredients to having a good conversation.

- *Connection.* The first ingredient is connection. You won't want to spend much time together unless you can create that environment where they know you care. Your relationship is about the person and not about a project. So, take the time to get to know the person. I like to ask simple, safe questions. I will say, I would love to hear your story. I will ask about where they grew up. How many were in their family? Who was their favorite teacher? What was a major challenge in their life and did that impact their life? Make it personal – slow down. Stop giving your attention to anything else. If you get to share your story, be honest. Honesty is part of the price you pay to have a good conversation. There is risk. But when you start, you are building trust. Risk will come much easier later when you have established trust.

- *Questions.* For the conversation to be interesting, ask open-ended questions. To state this clearly, avoid questions that can be answered with one word. I learned the importance of this when my kids were in high school. If you have had the privilege of raising teenagers, you may have had the same experience. I would ask, "Where are you going? I would get back, "Out." "Who are you going with?" "Friends." When will you get home? "Late." An open-ended question requires more thought on the other person's part. "What did you do?" "How did that work for you?" "Can you give me an example of what that looked like?" "Can you describe for me what that felt like?"

  I like good questions, and it is fun to collect them. John Maxwell likes to say that good leaders ask great questions. What great questions can you create?

- *Listen.* The third ingredient for moving the conversation from a chat to something profound—listen deeply. This is where you take listening from skill to art. As Stephen Covey has famously said in his book The *7 Habits of Highly Successful People,* "Seek first to understand, then to be understood."

Here are some rules for deep listening.
1. The first rule is to listen with your eyes. Observe that person. The research shows that over 90 percent of our communication is non-verbal. What is their body language? Are they excited? Is there energy? It might be that you see the pain in their expression even if the words don't

match the face. You will understand much more when you see the person and not just hear the words, leading to the next rule.

2. The second rule is to listen deeply by listening for the pain points in their story. When you are trusted with an honest expression of pain in their life, you have great opportunity to provide hope on their journey.

3. The third rule is to not interrupt, especially if the other person is upset. Sometimes our tendency is to want to make the person feel better as quickly as possible. We may want to interject some of our own stories too soon just to let them know that they are not alone. I advise you to be patient. Your opportunity will come. Let them tell their whole story before you tell yours.

4. The fourth rule is to acknowledge their emotions. It is appropriate to step in with a phrase like, "I can tell that hurt you." Or "You really enjoyed that, didn't you?" Let the person experience that your observation is deeper than just hearing the words coming out.

5. Fifth is to summarize. "Here is what I hear you saying. Am I getting it right?" This feedback ensures that the communication is accurate.

6. Finally, I would add as a rule: use silence. Don't be afraid of a little tension in the air. These are moments for personal insights to take deeper root and prepare for deep

change. This deep change that I keep talking about comes from a strategic journey that includes the right conversations at the right time.

Next, we will talk about the first conversation: The Integrity Conversation.

But before we go there, it is possible that you might be saying "I don't know how to…"

Let me remind you of my time back in that driver's ed car. The message still rings true.

Let's slow down. Hear my voice: "You can do this."

CHAPTER 2: I DON'T KNOW HOW TO DRIVE

Questions for Reflection

1. Can you describe a time when you felt fearful, but went ahead and did what you needed to? What did you learn from that experience?

2. What skill have you developed over time? How did you develop that skill?

3. Can you give an example of a time you listened deeply?

I Think We Missed Something, Part 1

> "Telling the truth starts with
> knowing where you are."
> — Anonymous

The Integrity Conversation

*I*t is impossible to know you are moving in the right direction if you don't know where you are.

All six of us started confidently. It was 1992 and summer on the Olympic Peninsula. The clouds were beginning to burn off, and the morning was chilly when we were dropped off at the beginning of the Skokomish South Fork Trailhead. The backpacking hike would take us over Sundown Pass so we could camp overnight at Lake Sundown. The plan for the second day was to keep walking above Graves Creek and eventually end up in the Quinault River valley where we would be picked up. Our company of six was made up of my two brothers-in-law, two young nephews, my thirteen-year-old son and me. I was ready with my backpack, optimism and new hiking boots that were already slightly uncomfortable.

Our first day was challenging. The map shows we walked 7.51 miles, but it felt a lot farther. Much of the path was easy to follow as we followed the river. But as we headed for the pass, the path changed, zig zagging up steep terrain. I started a joke that I was "baby stepping" through the switchbacks. The movie "What About Bob" was new that year.

Some of my clear memories include the Elk herd that kept moving to keep the trees between us and them. Eventually, we trudged over the pass and down to the lake, caught fish and slept soundly from exhaustion.

The next day we headed west and then north toward Wynoochee Pass. As planned, we skipped our turn to Wynoochee continuing north on the Graves Creek Trail. If you study the map closely, it is called the Graves Creek Primitive Trail. It is called primitive because the trail is not marked much of the way. There are no signs, and the path can look more like a deer trail if you can find it.

When we couldn't see the path, we would stop and look for Forest Service ribbons tied to trees. When we saw a ribbon, we would move toward it. Either a new ribbon would appear on another tree for us to follow or we would rediscover the path. This all worked fine until we couldn't find a path or a ribbon. As we searched, I saw a ribbon fairly far away, tied to a tree, up the steep hill.

I climbed up to it, and the others followed. We saw another ribbon, again far away up the hill. These ribbons were only slightly different in appearance than the previous trail ribbons. We followed up with a few more. The already steep slope was getting steeper. And then there was no ribbon. We were in the middle of the forest. To be more accurate, we were lost, and we didn't know where we were or which way to go. Standing lost on the mountainside was a humbling experience for three grown men, trying to look brave for our three young men. It was worse than humbling. We were tired, inexperienced, lost and starting to fight the fear creeping in.

Together, we assessed the situation and decided we had missed something. We agreed to go back down the mountainside, following the ribbons again to find the last place we were confident we had been on the trail. We found where we had stopped before. Once there, we took more time to look for trail clues. It wasn't long before we searched the other side of a large bolder that had caused our original stop. There we found the trail again and we were on our way. Ten more miles on a well-worn path and we found our ride.

Where Are You?

For decades I have pondered about getting lost on that trip. How easy it was to get off track. How being tired probably added to our hasty decision to go uphill, even though it seemed counterintuitive. Being lost is an awful feeling. Realizing that when you don't know where you are, you don't know how to head in the right direction to get out of trouble.

Our first conversation to reach Uncommon Success is the Integrity Conversation. In this conversation we are seeking to answer the question "Where are you?" If you do not know where you are, it is impossible to know what your next step will be to move in a positive direction.

This is the conversation that asks for your compass points in key areas of life. It is vital that you tell the truth, as best as you can, when you explore where you are in these areas.

Grounded Reality

Honesty can be difficult in those moments when it is most needed. But it brings advantages of simplicity and freedom. Dishonesty is harder because it lingers in the back of the mind. It can take on a life of its own and where you're at as you try and remember what you've said. You try and stay consistent with what you've said, but if it is not true, there is a disconnect with reality. Mark Twain wrote, "Always tell the truth. That way you don't have to remember what you said." There is wisdom in his words.

The kind of truth I am talking about I call *grounded reality*. It is real. Grounded in truth. As the philosopher/theologian Francis Shaeffer used to say, "True Truth." To live with grounded reality means we do not shade the truth. We do not spin our stories to make ourselves look better. There is good news here. We are not opening ourselves up for everyone to look deep into our lives.

This is not the time for a public confession of our faults. What we mean is that true truth is for our self-development. Telling the truth to yourself about your whole life sets you free to grow. It gives you a clear picture of where you are. It lets you know what direction to take to get on a safe and productive path.

CHAPTER 3: I THINK WE MISSED SOMETHING, PART 1

The Integrity Trap — Almost True Stu

On this journey to experience Uncommon Success, we discover there are common traps where people get stuck. The trap that hinders integrity is almost telling the truth, and we have named the victim of this trap Almost True Stu.

Have you met Stu? He is very good at painting nice pictures of his life. He doesn't talk much about his frustrations or confusion. One of his favorite words is "fine." Stu often says, "Everything is fine." But he may really be Frustrated, Irritated, Nervous and Exhausted.

If Stu got lost on the same hike we took, he would say he had a nice walk, explored some areas off the path, and it was all great. You wouldn't know he was fearful. You wouldn't know that he was concerned for his son and the rest of the party. Those feelings may have been a very real and a significant part of his experience. But he just wouldn't mention them. Very few Stu's have anyone in their lives who will confront them about half-truths.

Let's be clear. We are not talking about having a positive attitude at this point. While managing one's attitude is an important skill, we are talking about Stu being honest with Stu.

Some of the more common feelings that are associated with this trap are frustration, confusion, denial and fear. And the issue isn't just having those feelings: it's being stuck in those feelings without knowing how to move through them.

Getting out of this trap requires a few steps.

1. Find a strategic mentor you trust for Integrity Conversation. This is the most important. A person looking to do the work of deep change will need a healthy guide. Other steps will fall into place once you have your

trusted mentor. The mentor does not need to have a perfect life. While they may have some experience, their important role will be to carefully listen and offer genuine feedback.

2. Be prepared to do the work of soul-searching. This is an opportunity to reflect deeply about what is true and what is not true about your life. The more honest you can be about where you are in life, the faster you can make adjustments to the direction you are headed.

3. Use the TARGET Assessment to begin to tell yourself the truth about yourself. This assessment is meant as a general guide. It becomes more valuable as you commit to grounded reality and begin the work toward hitting TARGET. The chart will be explained after walking through the assessment.

TARGET ASSESSMENT

Directions: This assessment usually takes about 1 hour to complete. We don't want you to feel like you need to hurry. Going faster or slower is entirely up to you. We suggest you find a quiet place where you can think. Do not feel confined by the space provided on the form. You can write as much as you would like. Take your time thinking through your answers to the questions. This assessment is for your benefit. Be as honest as possible. If you are not sure about an answer, go ahead and say so. If you skip any questions, be sure to go back and complete those questions.

Once you have completed the form, return it to your Strategic Mentor and schedule your Assessment Review appointment.

Remember you are at the beginning of a great adventure. Have Fun!

General Direction

1. Describe what you would like to accomplish in the next 90 days. 1 year. 3 years.

2. What is your main motivation for wanting to make changes?

3. Can you tell me about a time in your life when you felt your life was working well? What has changed?

4. Explain any concerns regarding your health.

5. What concerns, challenges or problems might affect your ability to participate in the process of strategic mentoring?

Life Tools – Finances and Time

6. Do you know the balance in your bank account? Circle one: Yes / No. (We do not need the amount.)

7. Do you have a financial plan? Yes / No

8. Do you feel that you understand money? Yes / No. Please explain.

9. How would you describe your mindset toward money?

10. Do you currently have a written budget? Yes / No. If "yes", do you follow it consistently? Yes/No. What are 2 or 3 challenges you face in following your budget?

11. Do you plan your days ahead of time? Yes / No (circle one)

12. If yes, how do you go about planning your day and your week? List any tools or strategies you use.

13. Please describe how you use your first 90 minutes of your workdays.

Life Skill – Attitude

14. On a scale of 1-10 (with 1 low and 10 high), how would you rate your overall outlook on life right now? Please explain:

15. On a scale of 1-10, How would you rate your sense of fulfillment? Please explain:

16. On a scale of 1-10, How would you rate your sense of:

    - Joy?
    - Happiness?
    - Peace?

17. On a scale of 1-10, what would you consider your level of worry? (Is worry impacting your life?)

18. On a scale of 1-10, what would you consider your level of stress?

19. Please describe your favorite kind of humor.

Life Skill – Relationships

20. Describe your family of origin, (parents, siblings, where you fit in). If you are married, describe your marriage(s), kids etc.

21. Do you feel like you have close friends? Yes / No

    If you answer "Yes", describe why they are close to you.

    If you answer "No", why do you believe that to be true?

22. Do you consider yourself a "relational person" or more of a "task person"?

23. Do you consider yourself a "fast pace" person or more of a "steady pace" person?

Life Skill – Grace

24. Do you find it easy to forgive? Can you give an example when forgiveness came easy to you?

25. Can you give an example of when you experienced forgiveness?

26. Self-esteem can be defined as feeling that you are lovable and capable. On a scale of 1-10, how would you score your self-esteem? Please explain your score.

27. On a scale of 1-10, How important are others' opinions of you? Please explain your score.

Life Skill – Energy

28. What are you doing when you tend to lose track of time?

29. Do you have any hobbies? Please describe them.

30. If you had absolute freedom, what would you love to do? (If time and finances were not a barrier.)

31. How would you describe your Core Genius? (What do you believe you love and do better than other people?)

32. What is your level of activity each week? Can you describe the quality and quantity of activity?

33. How many hours of sleep do you regularly enjoy? Can you describe both the quality and quantity of your sleep?

34. On a scale of 1-10, what is the level of your energy each day? Please explain.

CHAPTER 3: I THINK WE MISSED SOMETHING, PART 1

Life Skills – Transformation Plan

35. Do you have any written goals? If so, are they SMART goals?

36. Do you know what your "Breakthrough Goal" is? Please describe it here.

37. What have you done in the past to create change in your life?

38. On a scale of 1-10, how successful were you in your effort? Please explain what worked for you and what did not work.

39. Please explain any strategic life planning you have done in the past?

I Think We Missed Something, Part 2

"Telling the truth starts with knowing where you are"
— Anonymous

The Integrity Conversation

Now that you have walked through the TARGET Assessment, it is time to evaluate where you are. On the chart below, you will see both Success and Significance with arrows moving from lower to higher. Everyone wrestles with these drives. Through the years we have noticed that people tend to be driven by one more than the other. One is not right and the other wrong. It is just a matter of how you are personally wired. After thinking through your Assessment, how would you rate yourself on the arrow of Success? Would you consider yourself higher or lower on the axis?

Then ask yourself where you consider yourself on the Significance arrow.

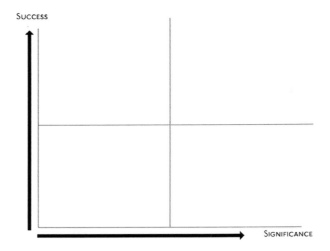

Where those two dots intersect on the chart is your assessment of where you are currently.

For example, if you believe you are higher on the success axis than the significance axis, you might place a mark like the top illustration on the next page.

CHAPTER 4: I THINK WE MISSED SOMETHING, PART 2

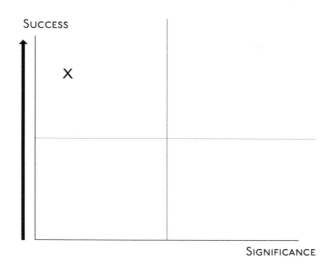

Or you may find yourself driven more by Significance and see yourself lower on the Success side. Then you might see your intersection point looking like the illustration below.

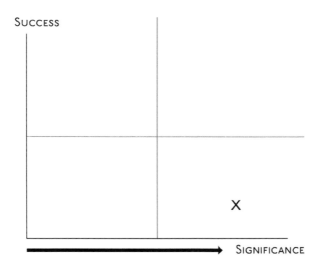

You will also notice that we have divided the chart into 4 quadrants. Each quadrant identifies key feelings with being in that quadrant. Below you can see three examples of feelings that might go with the quadrant.

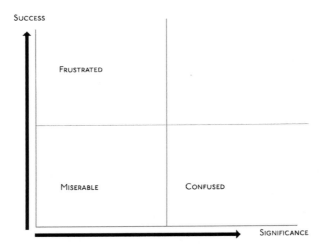

It is easy to see if you are feeling higher on the Success axis but lower in significance how that might feel frustrating. Because you have so much going for you from one perspective, but you do not feel like it is very meaningful. You may be asking, what is the point of it all?

Also, you can see how a person who spends their time in significant endeavors, but struggles financially and to pay the bills, might feel confused. They are giving so much of themselves in service, why is that not being rewarded?

If a person is scoring low in both categories, it is not a stretch to imagine that life isn't working, and they could feel miserable.

CHAPTER 4: I THINK WE MISSED SOMETHING, PART 2

Our goal in Strategic Mentoring is to move everyone we work with into the 4th quadrant. We call that the TARGET Box. Each letter of TARGET highlights an area for growth, on the journey to an integrated, holistic, and healthy life.

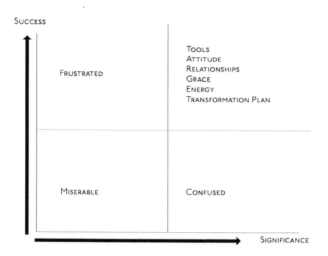

As a Strategic Mentor, the goal of the Integrity conversation is to help a person know, as objectively as possible, where they are in life. And then begin to help that person on the journey toward living on TARGET. This is a good time to remind you that, by *the 5 Conversations*, we are talking about five types of conversations. The first is the Integrity Conversation and that conversation will include transformative actions to help a person grow in these six areas.

1. T – Tools. When we talk about tools, we mean the basics of Time, Talent and Treasure. How is the mentee doing

with managing their time? Does the mentee know what they do well and should be focusing upon? Does the mentee understand their finances? These are all areas to grow in. As a person grows in those, they are moving toward becoming "On TARGET."

2. A – Attitude. It is well understood that attitude is a key determinant in how successful a person will become. Managing our attitude is a skill that takes time and significant awareness. This is an area where I had to make a major adjustment. Years ago, before I began this journey, I was one who tended to whine when things weren't working out for me. I remember very clearly when I started learning the lessons of the top motivational teachers. It was apparent they were all teaching the same truth in a variety of ways. The truth is, "You do not get healthy until you take 100 percent responsibility for your own life." We will talk more about this when we get to the Productivity Conversation.

3. R – Relationships. Many people measure their success through things like houses, clothes, cars and vacations. In Strategic Mentoring, we help people learn to measure their success through their relationships. Becoming more skilled in your relationships brings much greater fulfillment than owning a newer car. We will discuss this more in the Identity Conversation.

4. G – Grace. We are talking about common grace here rather than divine grace. Are you a forgiving person not

only toward others but also toward yourself? This will be addressed in more depth in the Identity and Authenticity Conversations. The key to making grace a part of your life is to move away from judgment of others. A simple exercise is to try and go one day without judging another person or even yourself. You may come to realize how much you need to be intentional about pursuing a grace filled life.

5. E – Energy. There are two key questions that get addressed as we look at energy. First, how is your health? Second is, what is it that really gives you energy?

   The first question has to do with all the physical aspects of your life. How is your weight? Do you eat a healthy diet? Are you staying well hydrated? Are you getting exercise? Are you getting enough sleep? These are very important questions to maintain your physical energy.

   The second question has to do with your motivation. Are you using your motivated abilities? Do you know what you love to do? Do you have time to do it? Do you know what is expected of you at work? Do you have the resources and tools to do that work? What is it that you are doing when you lose track of time? We will return to Energy in Identity and Authenticity Conversations.

6. T – Transformation Plan. All great projects start with a plan. You will be making personal adjustments as you work through the 5 Conversations. A template for

creating your own transformational plan for personal growth and development is available on the website www.stevenbwelling.com.

Uncommon Success

Begin to notice the power of the 5 Conversations. They are not designed to just get you to experience life on TARGET. Rather, this process is designed for continued improvement. It is a process that can be repeated time after time and help people grow through different barriers. If you know where you are, you can keep moving to the upper right quadrant of the upper right quadrant always moving toward mastering Uncommon Success. You continue to grow and grow, becoming a person who is worth knowing and less concerned about being well known. Once the foundation of Integrity is established, you are ready for the next conversation.

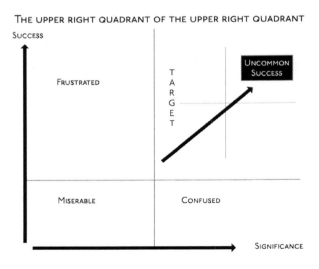

CHAPTER 4: I THINK WE MISSED SOMETHING, PART 2

Questions for Reflection

1. Can you describe a situation when you shaded the truth to make things appear better than they were?

2. Why do you believe a grounded reality level of honesty is so difficult?

3. Can you chart yourself on the TARGET Assessment? What is one thing you can do to make a positive move?

Is That You?

> "The simplest questions can take
> the longest to answer."
> — Anonymous

The Identity Conversation — Who am I?

The other day, a three-year-old boy I know saw me in a different context. I am a neighbor to his grandparents, and we've seen each other numerous times. At first, he didn't recognize me; I was wearing a hat and sunglasses while watching my grandson play baseball at school. His brother plays on the same team as my grandson. We were all there enjoying the game when he looked at me, pondered for a moment, and asked, "Is that you?"

That is a simple question. And yet one people wrestle with through a lifetime.

Is that you? Or we ask ourselves, "Who am I?" There is amazing depth to the question. It is one of those questions that follow us. Socrates said, "To know thyself is the beginning of wisdom." He also said, "The unexamined life is not worth living." Greek philosophy is often quoted with the key advice, "Know thyself."

The Bible teaches, "The fear of the Lord is the beginning of wisdom; all who follow his precepts have good understanding" (Psalm 111:10, NIV).

We are to have examined lives. The Apostle Paul writes to the church in Rome, "For by the grace given me I say to every one of you: Do not think of yourself more highly than you ought, but rather think of yourself with sober judgment" (Rom 12:3a, NIV). Just as we are not to think more highly, we should not think less of ourselves either. We need to have a clear image of ourselves. Identity is the way we truly see ourselves and it is powerful. Tony Robbins says, "Identity is the most important power that determines our actions. We will act according to our views of who we truly are—whether these views are accurate or not."

What Is Personal Identity?

When we begin the exploration of personal identity, it is the beginning of a long journey.

In the research literature, you will see a list of traits that make up a person's identity: race, ethnicity, sexual orientation, ability, religion/spirituality, nationality, and socioeconomic status.

We can add to that age, family of origin, education, life experience and self-esteem. More factors could be added. The important thing to see is that everything in life adds to our identity. But the most important factor in shaping our identity is in our mind. It is the story we tell and believe about ourselves. Therefore, the goal of the Identity conversation is to help others personally define themselves with integrity.

Two Traps: Borrowing Betty and Conformin' Norman

Two common traps that people fall victim to in the search for personal identity are borrowing and blending.

After a phone call with my mother, I sat there a little dumbfounded. My mother had asked me again, "What is it that you do?" We had this conversation earlier that year when I made the transition from being a pastor to working as a management consultant and corporate trainer.

The explanation was, "As consultant, I work with management teams to identify root causes of problems, usually with processes or staffing. We will then explore solutions and develop strategies to implement those solutions. In other words, I go to a lot of meetings, listen to a lot of people and help them become more productive." I went on from there to give her the details.

I can't say with confidence all the details of what I shared. What I do remember very clearly was her reply after my overlong and complex answer to her simple question. When I was finished, she asked, "Do you mind if I just tell my friends you are a pastor?" There it was. The real issue was out on the table. My mother had spent over twenty years of her life answering the question from her friends, "What is Steve doing now?" For years my mother could say that her son was a pastor. She was happy to say it. It was easy. It was succinct. She could say it proudly.

The work of consulting didn't fit her view of me. It turned out that my work helped shape her own identity. She was borrowing from my identity. She was a Borrowing Betty.

There is a danger for all of us that we allow our identity to be shaped by others and not have a self-defined picture of ourselves. When our identity is dependent on the identity of others, our world shifts by the actions of another.

The irony was that I was having as much difficulty with my identity as my mother. I spent years in college and graduate school preparing for the pastorate. Pastoral roles had become a part of my life since the mid-1970s. Now it was 1999, and I was working outside of my comfort zone. It was a new world. Many of the skills were similar. However, I was no longer using my Reverend title. I felt like a stranger in a strange land. Just a regular guy.

Unaware, I had fallen victim to the second trap of identity. I operated as a Conformin' Norman, spending years blending into my environment, keeping the peace. You could say I was laying low, playing it safe. In my leadership responsibilities, I often borrowed ideas from other successful leaders. Why take a risk?

Woody Allen, in his 1983 movie "Zelig" tells the story of a Conformin' Norman. He is the ultimate blending trap victim. Set in the 1920s and 1930s, the film concerns Leonard Zelig (Woody Allen), a nondescript man who has the ability to transform his appearance to that of the people who surround him. He is first observed at a party by F. Scott Fitzgerald, who notes that Zelig related to affluent guests in a refined Boston accent and shared their Republican sympathies, but while in the kitchen with the servants, he adopted a coarser tone and seemed to be more of a Democrat. He soon gained international fame as a "human chameleon."[4] This is a very creative way to describe the life of a person who is not self-defined.

As strategic mentors, our goal in the identity conversation is to help others avoid borrowing and blending to their detriment. It isn't healthy being a human chameleon instead of becoming our most authentic self.

Keys to Developing a Healthy Personal Identity

How do we answer the question, "Who am I?" And how do we do so in a productive way? I view it as a journey of deep soul work rather than a destination. This journey is a challenge because our identity can keep changing as we grow and mature. With new experiences, we are recalibrating our self-perception all the time. Every victory, every loss, every celebration, every disappointment will bring new data to the equation. In one sense, we are in a perpetual state of reinventing ourselves. If you get frustrated along the way, remember the Chinese proverb by Lao Tzu: "A journey of a thousand miles begins with a single step."

There are powerful tools available to you to do this deep work, and I rely on three major components to get to the heart of who you are. I call this checking your Identity CPR. C stands for Cultivate your Self-Esteem. P reminds us to Practice Profile Awareness. R encourages us to use Reflection to go deeper as we recalibrate our lives.

C – Cultivate your Self-Esteem

Self-esteem is interesting because it is often misunderstood. Some people argue that self-esteem is a way of exalting "self." I believe they confuse self-esteem with self-image. Self-image is the way you see yourself. Self-esteem is the way you feel about yourself. They each are a part of personal identity. The problem with self-image is when it becomes more important than character. That is when we see people busy themselves with image maintenance. They are so busy worrying about how others view them that they spend their timed focused on the externals. They are not necessarily worried about what they wear or look like. Rather they are more concerned about what others will think of what they wear or their appearance. We live in a culture that emphasizes the externals. Spend any time looking at magazines, or watch award shows on television, you don't find much interest in character traits. But you do find a lot of information on the latest fashions of those people we now call influencers.

In contrast, self-esteem in the best sense is a gift that you give to yourself, free from the opinions of others. A simple way to define self-esteem is with the acrostic IALAC which stands for: I Am Lovable and Capable. Self-esteem is built on the foundation of believing you are worthy of love and that you are competent in life. As a general rule, most people are very hard on themselves. We each tend to be our worst critic. If we take the path of the culture, in looking for our value and acceptance through our external appearance, we will forever be chasing the wind.

I once spent an entire week with Jack Canfield working on my own self-esteem and learning how to encourage others on the journey. Here are a few techniques you can use to cultivate your self-esteem.

CHAPTER 5: IS THAT YOU?

1. My Success Exercise. Using a sheet of paper, divide your life into three equal periods. (i.e., birth-15, 16-30, 31-45) and list three successes for each period on the sheet. After that, list three successes you would like to have in the next five years.

2. Use the Mirror Exercise. This is a stretch for many people, but don't let that stop you from trying it. This exercise helps change negative beliefs you may have about yourself and shifts your mind toward love and acceptance. It is suggested that you practice this for 30 to 90 days before you decide how you feel about it.

    To practice the mirror exercise, stand in front of a mirror before you go to bed. Look at yourself directly in the eye. Speak out loud addressing yourself by name and begin appreciating yourself. Congratulate yourself for any positive accomplishments that day. Give yourself credit for any disciplines that you have kept—exercise, journaling, diet, reading, prayer etc. Acknowledge any temptations you avoided—eating too much, watching too much TV, allowing your phone to overly distract you.

    The goal here is to look deep into your own eyes and love yourself sincerely. You can even say to yourself, "I love you." If God loves you, so can you.

3. Learn the power of E + R = O. When leading seminars, I almost always include this teaching. Jack Canfield taught me this, and it revolutionized my life.[5] The formula works this way.

- H stands for Events.
- R stands for Response.
- O stands for Outcomes.

Life events plus our response equals the outcome. Events by definition are things that you cannot control. It could be the weather, the sun coming up or someone cutting you off in traffic. You cannot control those things. In fact, you cannot control almost everything you experience in life other than your response. If you don't like the outcomes you are getting in life, using this formula will give you guidance. Think about this. Outcomes are a combination of events plus your response, and the only thing you can change in the formula is your response. You become empowered when you realize there is always a way to change the outcome, by changing your response.

In the Integrity conversation, I said that we would talk about relationships in this conversation. Think about how practicing E+R=O could change your relationships for the better.

What is interesting is that our responses are based on our thoughts. This is why it is so important to understand this in the context of our conversation about identity and self-esteem. For example, let's say you are standing in line at Starbucks and a guy behind you starts telling you to hurry up and make your order. But you can't decide if you want a Grande Mocha or a triple shot Americano. While you ponder your decision, he calls you a big jerk. Now you have a choice to make. Remember the formula:

Event (guy is pushy and calls you a jerk) + Response (you turn and let him know he is the real jerk) = Outcome (a shouting match and still no one has coffee).

But there is a choice. It might work this way. The event (guy is pushy and calls you a jerk) + different responses (You turn and smile and say sorry that you are having a hard time. You could let him go ahead of you. You could offer to pay for his drink.)

It doesn't matter how you respond. Just notice that you have a choice of how to respond. With a different response, you will create a different outcome. Here is what we need to understand. It is not the guy calling you a jerk that causes your response. It is what you say to yourself after he has said it that causes your response. If he calls you a jerk and in your mind, you say, "Yes, I am a jerk. How did he find out so fast?" This will create a more confrontive outcome. If you were to say it to yourself, "He doesn't know me. I am a decent guy." Your response will be different and will create a different outcome. The point here is that, when we are clear on our identity and have a healthy self-esteem, we can respond to life in a much more positive way.

Give yourself the gift of self-esteem. You are the only one who can.

P – Practice Profile Awareness

The next tool in the box for building a healthy sense of identity is to use profiles. There are many kinds of profiles to help us understand how we tend to operate. There are behavioral profiles like the Portrait Predictor from the Strategic Team-Makers, a DISC behavioral profile or Myers-Briggs Type Indicator. There are many quadrant systems out there as well that are easy to use.

Another type of profile is Clifton Strengthsfinder, made available through the Gallup company. It is more of a talent assessment. Through their research, they have identified 34 strengths that people bring to the workplace. You can identify your top talents and leverage them into strengths to help you find more joy and satisfaction in work and home.

Earlier we talked about understanding what energizes us. I have used Strengthsfinder for years and have found it very helpful in understanding what some call motivated abilities. It was Strengthsfinder that helped me the most to understand why I had burned out in one church. After studying my results, I realized that what I did best, the church didn't necessarily want. And what the church needed most was not what I liked to do. Of course, we didn't go into that pastorate knowing that. Later, it was through this tool and a few others that allowed me the freedom to leave that ministry and recover from burnout. Once I understood my talents, I began to refine them to turn them into strengths. The talents become strengths when they are productively applied. Once I understood my strengths, I never made another decision on work without thinking through how they would be used. I learned the kind of activity that leverages my talents. When I was able to productively apply those talents, they became my strengths. Now, when I have the opportunity to work from my strengths, I am energized. I can work for hours in my strength and completely lose track of time.

A different kind of tool that goes after the same understanding of motivated abilities is called SIMA. That is short for the System for Identifying Motivated Abilities.

A third type of profile that is very helpful comes from the Barrett Values Center. Their profiling system reveals a person's motivating values. Building your work around clear personal values can be very rewarding.

Most coaches or mentors have some access to these types of tools. You will want to ask about their preferred profiles when you work on them.

R – Recalibrate Through Deep Reflection

Working through and develop a clear understanding of your identity can be a lot of work. And a lot of that work is a reflection on your past. But here is a word of caution on the topic of reflection: It is possible to get bogged down looking back.

A man considered the wisest person who ever lived tells us, "This is what I have observed to be good: that it is appropriate for a person to eat, to drink and to find satisfaction in their toilsome labor under the sun during the few days of life God has given them—for this is their lot. Moreover, when God gives someone wealth and possessions, and the ability to enjoy them, to accept their lot and be happy in their toil—this is a gift of God. *They seldom reflect on the days of their life, because God keeps them occupied with gladness of heart*" (Ecclesiastes 5:18-20, NIV, emphasis mine).

We learn here that life is to be enjoyed. While it is valuable to reflect, it is important that we don't get stuck in a cycle of reliving the past that we can't change. We use reflection to learn and move our lives forward. The goal is to experience what Solomon calls "A heart of gladness." Here are ten reflection questions that help explore facets of identity and move toward a heart of gladness.

1. What matters most in my life?

2. Who has had the greatest impact on my life? How?

3. What's the one thing I'd like others to remember about me at the end of my life?

4. Am I holding on to something I need to let go of?

5. What did I want to be when I was growing up?

6. What is my passion in life?

7. What is my favorite picture of myself and why?

8. What is one thing I would like to change about myself and why?

9. What do you fear most?

10. How do I want to be remembered at the end of my life?

Who am I? A simple question that leads to robust thought and conversation. Clarity around our personal identity moves us toward our goal of Uncommon Success by giving us a deeper understanding of our unique design. After we know where we are and who we are, we move to the question, "Where am I going?" That takes us to our next chapter – The Vision Conversation.

Questions for Reflection

1. How have you explored your uniqueness in the past?

2. Can you give an example of being tempted to just blend in instead of speaking from your true self?

3. Why do you think it is important to understand your personal identity?

Living with Vision

"Your vision will become clear only when you look into your heart. Who looks outside dreams? Who looks inside, awakens."
— Anonymous

The Vision Conversation — Where are you going?

There is nothing quite like looking at someone else's pictures. I have a full album. Let me show you just a few snapshots where I caught a glimpse of my life vision.

Snapshot 1: Spokane WA

Sitting in the back of a van with the rest of the college cross country team on our way to Eastern Oregon University to race the next day. I am a Junior and need to make decisions about what to study for my future. Over two years into college, and I am on my path to become a teacher with an education major. Recently, I am feeling compelled to prepare for seminary. I have to make a decision about next year. Would I follow through with a student teaching assignment? Or will I enroll in the Greek class to prepare for ministry? Due to circumstances, I can't do both. What should I do?

Somewhere in the Blue Mountains of Oregon, I sensed that I should take Greek. That decision set me on a ministry path covering the next five years. Was it a calling? I had a glimpse of a vision for the next step of my life.

Snapshot 2: St. Paul MN

I am living in Minnesota, finishing up my studies with a Master of Divinity degree. Statistics show that most seminary graduates find their first assignment within a 200-mile radius of the school. As graduation approaches, I am feeling compelled that I should move my small family 1500 miles back to the Pacific Northwest.

We made the move. Was this move a conviction to my calling or a commitment to my vision for ministry in the Northwest? I had a glimpse of what I was made for. Relocating didn't immediately open doors to the ministry; instead, I worked for the State of Washington. I spent a year interviewing welfare recipients before I accepted a position in a church. I wondered if my vision was a mistake.

Snapshot 3: Seattle WA

It doesn't make sense anymore. Twenty years of ministry, and now all I feel is tired. The bi-vocational work of the last two years is providing well for my family. I love traveling around the country leading seminars. I am not excited or deeply motivated to return to church on weekends to preach and lead. What should I do? Can I really leave the ministry? Is that allowed? What about my calling?

I handed my resignation to the board. It was official; I was becoming an entrepreneur. I was starting my own consulting and training business. Was this God's leading? I felt compelled to leave professional ministry as clearly as I had been called twenty-five years earlier. Where had my vision for ministry in the Northwest gone? Maybe this is what they call the death of a vision. There is certainly a glimpse of confusion.

Snapshots 4: Kirkland WA

Sitting in his office, the pastor looks at me and casually says, "I want you to come on board and be a part of our staff. It may take some time to work out, but we would like you to be a part of the ministry team here." After five years of independence, is this what I am supposed to do? Is this how I am supposed to serve again? Is this another glimpse of my vision for ministry in the Northwest?

Snapshot 5: Houston TX

On the road again. Today, I am sitting in the back of a rental car. The other seminar leaders are in front driving and talking about work and life at home. My cell phone rings. "When can you start?" Am I ready for this? This is starting to feel like a pattern. The sense of discomfort leading me to pray. The questions are different now. I think more about my identity as I weigh the opportunity. Am I a pastor? Would this position allow me to do what I do well? How does this decision affect my family? I feel compelled to accept a ministry opportunity. The transition didn't take long, and I felt right at home with new responsibilities.

Snapshot 6: Seattle WA

What have I learned about vision? Here I sit in this nice office. I can't believe it has been over sixteen years since I stepped back into ministry. I can't believe how I am able to provide leadership to ministries all over the Pacific Northwest. I enjoy my work encouraging and developing leaders. I enjoy the constant travel. I think it is time to transition. I believe I fulfilled my calling. I believe I lived out my vision from over 40 years ago.

About now, you may be like the guy sitting in the back row of church watching too many missionary slides of people whose names he can't remember. He was heard to ask in a stage whisper, "Where's the sunset?"

CHAPTER 6: LIVING WITH VISION

Vision — One Glimpse at a Time

Admittedly, "vision" is a slippery subject. It is one of those big ideas that people talk about but have difficulty defining. Different people may call it different things. Business coach, Brian Tracy, describes a person's vision by knowing one's Major Definite Purpose. Success author and coach Jack Canfield uses more tangible language. He says, "Your vision is a detailed description of where you want to get to." He adds that, "Your vision needs to include the following seven areas: work and career, finances, recreation and free time, health and fitness, relationships, personal goals, and contribution to the larger community."

I view vision as a combination of those two ideas. It definitely has a future orientation as suggested by Canfield. But it also includes understanding Tracy's definition that gets at personal uniqueness and purpose. For many, the term "Calling" moves close to the concept. But it is more than answering, "What am I called to do?" It includes, "What am I uniquely called to accomplish with my life?"

Through the years, I've wanted clarity about what my vision should be. In the photos I showed you, I kept coming back to the issue of my vision. But was it really clear at the time? I have many other photos of my life that would show you more confusion and frustration with the issue. On numerous occasions, I remember saying, "I just want clarity." It didn't come. Instead, what I got was glimpses of a vision. I had to make decisions on whether to pursue the glimpse with a heart of faith.

There are reports of some people like Joan of Arc. She had her vision, and her course was set. If you are one of the fortunate ones who has established your vision, own it and act on it.

Congratulations!

Most of us have to sort through countless mental photographs to put the big picture of our lives together. As you summarize your own important snapshots, look for glimpses. You may have a portion of your calling. You may know what to do and not be clear about where you are going. It becomes easy to try and take shortcuts to claim a vision.

The Copycat Cal Trap

Pastor Bernie, the retired pastor I had succeeded, was sitting in the second row with his wife. He was extremely well respected by his former congregation. They were now living in another town and had come to visit the church as a surprise. Maybe someone knew, but if they did, they didn't tell me. I was intimidated. Ever since I had arrived on the scene, I had heard stories of his skill in the pulpit. I was in my early 30s and still working to find my voice as a speaker. I wasn't bad, I just wasn't experienced. Which is probably why I fell victim to the Copycat Cal trap.

I recently returned from a ministry retreat. The speaker was an emerging pastor and leader whose church was exploding with growth. His vision was built around reaching people with the gospel through a new strategy, which he called "seeker friendly." He was persuasive and I decided to adopt the strategy. One of the things he did was to create sermon topics that were more fascinating than my usual fare. Therefore, I changed my sermon titles to be more intriguing. I didn't talk to anyone about this shift in philosophy. I simply adopted it as my own. The church I was serving was very traditional, but that didn't dissuade me from trying new ideas.

On this particular Sunday morning, I had begun the experimentation with my newly copied ideas. My sermon title for the day was, "Is There Sex After Marriage?" I still remember the looks on the faces of the former pastor and his wife. They were wide eyed, and I knew I at least had their attention.

I was guilty on that day of copying a strategy from someone else's vision. It wasn't the only time I was guilty of falling into the same trap. Later, when I worked with a lot of different leaders and churches, I noticed that this was a common problem. Many others were trapped by Copycat Cal syndrome.

Why Is Capturing Vision Difficult?

The difficulty in capturing our unique vision can be due to at least three challenges: risk aversion, avoidance of effort and time crunch.

The first is based in fear. Risk aversion is the risk of being judged. There is a risk in exposing your vision. We all try and protect ourselves. Sometimes those that support us the most seek to protect us as well. I once told a mentor of mine that I was fulfilling my sense of vision that I had held for over twenty years. His advice to me was, "Don't tell anyone." He feared that others would judge me.

We risk embarrassment and our reputation if we fail. Notice these risks have to do with what other people think of us. To get past this, I like to say, "It is none of my business what other people think of me." That is obviously easier said than done. But it can be done.

One of my associates and I had recently been talking about this exact subject. When she exited Starbucks with her Venti Mocha, unfortunately, she tripped outside the windows where all the people were seated. She fell face down in front of the crowd inside. She told me later, as she was lying on the ground staring into the cement, she heard herself say, "It is none of my business what other people think of me." She got up, walked back into the store to spontaneous applause, and reordered her drink.

Risk aversion is less about self-protection and more about fear and image maintenance. It is easy to see why it is important to build and maintain our self-esteem. That part of the identity conversation lays the groundwork for this vision conversation.

Avoidance of effort can also be a cause of not finding vision. It is an easier path if we just copy the work of others. I also understand the motivation. You can see the great results that others are getting. When they articulate the reasons why they have made their decisions, it all sounds very logical.

Why should I spend a lot of time thinking about it when they have done such a good job? This is often a result of our third difficulty in vision development. We are all under a time crunch. There is more to do than there is time to do it. Why not borrow from the best and the brightest to save time?

Unfortunately, you cannot copy, borrow or steal a unique vision for your life. It takes time to think and reflect deeply about your unique role in this world. It takes patience to work through identifying the values, strengths and assets that make you uniquely you. And it takes courage to overcome the fears that arise when you risk living with a unique vision for your life.

What we need is a strategy for identifying our unique vision.

Attend the Vision Academy

Imagine you are walking onto a beautiful college campus. The sun is shining down on green, lush, manicured lawns. The tall mature maple trees are in full leaf. As you make your way through

CHAPTER 6: LIVING WITH VISION

the courtyard, you notice all the buildings around you are stately and well kept. It is your first day at the Vision Academy, and you are entering four Vision Classes.

The First Class: Vision 101 – Look Up

When you walk into the classroom, the first thing you see is an old-fashioned chalkboard. Written in white chalk are the words from Os Guiness: "No idea short of God's call can ground and fulfill the truest human desire for purpose and fulfillment."

The first lesson of Vision 101 is built on the Scripture Jeremiah 33:3, "Call to me and I will answer you. I'll tell you marvelous and wondrous things that you could never figure out on your own" (The Message Bible).

Whether you are a person of faith or not, the lessons of Vision 101 are learned in reflective seeking and meditation. Some people refer to this as tuning into your Higher Power or higher consciousness. Whatever terminology you choose, make this meditative experience productive for you. In my faith tradition, Jesus taught that we can be confident when going to God, asking for help. "Ask, and you will be given what you ask for. Seek and you will find. Knock, and the door will be opened. For everyone who asks, and receives. Anyone who seeks, finds. If only you will knock, the door will open" (Matthew 7:7-8, NIV).

During your seeking moments with the Creator, I encourage you to ask for four things:

1. A quiet heart. It is easy as you begin to become anxious. The more you quiet your spirit and the less you strive, the more open you are to hearing.

2. Clarity around your identity from the Identity Conversation. You have been shaped by the Creator with unique gifts, passions and experiences. How do these factor into a unique calling?

3. Wisdom in knowing who to believe. At the same time, also ask for wisdom to know who to graciously ignore. Not everyone tells us the truth about ourselves.

4. Understanding any clues that you have previously experienced, including insights into your glimpses that would guide you forward.

The Second Class: Vision 201 – Look In

As you walk into this classroom, the chalkboard has this written on it in the words of John Dewey: "We do not learn from experience. We learn from reflecting on experience."

After you spend time looking up wisdom and guidance, it is time for reflection. Here are some questions that I like to ask to evaluate my sense of vision. After you consider these questions, meet with a friend and discuss the same questions with them. You will be surprised what you learn as you do the exercise.

1. What is it that, when I do it, I lose track of time?

2. What am I truly passionate about?

3. What seems to come more easily to me than it appears to do for others?

4. Is what I am doing each day meaningful?

5. Why do I think I am here? Think figuratively or literally as you answer this.

6. If people asked me what my mission statement is, what would I say?

7. What do I need to know?

8. What am I pretending not to know?

9. What do I really believe I am supposed to accomplish with my life?

10. If I knew it was impossible to fail, what would I do with my life?

The Third Class: Vision 301 – Looking Out

Notice on the board today the words, "Vision has a destination."

Vision 301 class is about looking forward and writing down what you see. Jack Canfield calls this principle, "Decide what you want." The one thing you want to make sure you do when you look forward, deciding what you want, is to write it down. There is a faith element to this facet of vision. I believe God plants interests and ideas in our minds. As we release ourselves from fearing what others may say, and start saying what we want, we come closer to the visions that have been placed in us.

Here are some good writing exercises to help capture your unique vision.

1. Make a list of everything you want to see. Where in the world would you like to go? Are there cities, national parks, countries or parts of the world that interest you? Be sure to explain why you are interested in seeing those things. That may be where you catch a glimpse of a divine nudge.

2. Make a list of everything you dream of becoming. Who do you plan to be? How are you going to become that person? What holds you back from being that person today? What special skills, training or experiences do you need to acquire?

3. Make a list of everything you would like to do. Sometimes this is referred to as your bucket list. What do you want to do in your life before it is over?

4. Make a list of everything that you would like to have. You don't have to be a greedy person to want to have things. Pick out those things that are important to you. Why are they important to you? What meaning would it have for you if you had them?

5. My Perfect Life Exercise. Take a sheet of paper and begin to write down what your perfect life looks like in the future. You can describe the work you will be doing and the people you work with. You can write about where you live and what your house looks like. You can write about family relationships, cars, and vacations. Write about whatever you would need to have in place in order for your life to be perfect in the future.

CHAPTER 6: LIVING WITH VISION

For this exercise, you don't need to list a date for it to happen. This is not a goal list. This is a description of what your perfect life would look like.

I have experienced the power of this exercise. The first time I wrote out my perfect life was in 1998. In 2008, I moved into a new house that we had built on our desired location. When I moved my office, I found my Perfect Life description from 1998. In ten years, 90 percent of what I had envisioned had come true. The other 10 percent became true over the following ten years. Now I am in pursuit of my newest version of My Perfect Life.

You too want to have a clear picture of where you want to go. The clearer you can describe it, see it, almost feel it, the more likely you will see it.

Only one more class in the Vision Academy, and it is critical.

The Fourth Class: Vision 401 – Courage to Go

On today's blackboard is written the words, "Courage is the ignition of vision."

While thinking about vision lately, I realized that one key component of living a life of vision is courage. When I've failed to live out my vision, it usually is because my courage was weak.

Now the following is an odd example, but it does illustrate a point.

My wife and I were visiting the Como Park Zoo in St. Paul, Minnesota. We had been married less than a year, and my brother-in-law was there too, on a date with his future bride. As we wandered through the zoo, we found the lion cage housing seven or eight sleeping lions. This cage was old fashioned, and the lions were separated from us by metal bars. They didn't use windows or water barriers that newer zoos use now. For our safety, they had installed a metal railing that kept us from getting too close to the cage bars. My brother-in-law, bored with sleeping lions, picked up a nearby discarded popcorn box, reached over the rail and began to scrape the cage bars, shouting, "Wake up!" We all laughed and laughed because those sleeping lions were immune to the noise. He was ignored. They kept sleeping.

However, there was a lion in the back section of their enclosure that we could not see, and she was annoyed. In the blink of an eye, she leapt out of the dark, all the way across the cage, over the sleeping lions, and took the popcorn box out of my brother-in-law's hand. I can't tell you much more detail, because the moment the paw hit the box, I hit the ground running. In five seconds, I was fifty yards away before I came to my senses. I realized I was safe. What I didn't realize, but soon found out, was how quickly I left my wife behind. She hasn't let me forget about it over the past forty-five years.

In that flash of a leaping lion moment, my fight or flight response kicked in. The point is that courage is not automatic but staying safe is. Our fears are usually like caged lions. We may think that we have our fears tame and asleep; however, it is easy to forget when they surprise us and leap out of the dark.

When we capture a vision that is a combination of calling and compelling, it may be scary. It is scary to decide to live out your vision. It is even scarier to declare your vision. It is possible that your fight or flight response might kick in. But you won't be the first one that has had to develop and choose courage. Remember, as the LORD said to Joshua, "Have I not commanded you? Be strong and courageous. Do not be afraid; do not be discouraged, for the LORD your God will be with you wherever you go" (Joshua 1:9, NIV).

Do you have a photo album of vision pictures from your past?

If you walk through these steps and graduate from the Vision Academy, you will realize you can always add more photos as life goes on. I especially want to encourage anyone who may be thinking it is too late. Maybe you are thinking you are too old. I have wrestled with that thought as well. But I have decided to reframe my thoughts. Now I say, "No matter how old I am, I still have the rest of my life." That makes every day valuable as I live with my own vision.

Conclusion

When you know where you are, who you are, and where you are going, you can begin to make plans on how you are going to get there. That is where we are headed next with the Productivity Conversation. This Uncommon Success that we seek continues to get closer as we combine vision and productivity.

Questions for Reflection

1. Can you remember a time when you were driven by a vision?

2. Why do you think a copycat vision is easier than a personally crafted vision?

3. How would you describe the current vision you have for your life?

How Do They Know Where We Are Going?

> "You're going the wrong way."
> — Trains Planes and Automobiles

The Productivity Conversation

In the movie *Trains, Planes and Automobiles*, with Steve Martin and John Candy, there is a particular scene that illustrates a point I want to share with you. Two strangers have become partners as they attempt to get from New York to Chicago before Thanksgiving. When their flight is canceled in New York, they begin a painfully humorous trip across the country.

In this scene, Steve Martin is asleep. John Candy is driving a rental car and narrowly avoids a disaster, which causes him to pull off the freeway. When he drives back onto the freeway, he unknowingly goes in the wrong direction and heads into oncoming traffic.

People in cars going the same direction, but in the correct lane, begin yelling, "You're going the wrong way!"

Candy's response is, "How do they know where we're going?"

Candy and Martin drive on, into oncoming traffic, oblivious to the danger they are in. I have quoted the above line from the movie more times than I can count, because it is so often true.

My new Apple Maps was talking to me from my phone. When the app said to go left or right, I did it. I was a compliant driver, happy in the knowledge that I was being led by a trusted source. I was on my way to meet with a leader who was walking through some difficulties. It is not easy to be that guy: I know from experience. In my difficult days, I found comfort from meeting with people who had more experience than I did. Now I was the voice of experience, and I didn't want to make him wait. I was running a little behind, but I was making good time.

Something seemed off when I made the last right turn. My trusted digital guide had me moving away from civilization and going past pastures with cows. A reassuring synthetic voice calmed my fears, saying my Starbucks destination was one mile away and would be on the left. Surely civilization would return in the next mile. One mile later that same voice announced that I had arrived. Unfortunately, I had arrived at a different pasture with different cows. Civilization was nowhere in sight. I double checked the address. I had written it correctly into the app.

After a brief phone call to the leader, who was sitting at a Starbucks about five miles from my location, I began the corrected course back to my meeting. I read later that someone at Apple got fired after that software update.

Sometimes we mistakenly go the wrong direction, and it is dangerous. Maybe we have made some bad decisions and didn't know it. Or we found out it was a bad decision but didn't take any action to correct it, even when we had been warned. Sometimes we follow bad advice. The information we were working with was wrong. Maybe we trusted the wrong voice. Whatever reason we have for going the wrong way, the important thing is to stop, recalibrate and move forward going the right way.

In this chapter, we are going to see the importance of positive productivity, meet the villainous gang of distractors that keep us from being productive and learn how to become much more productive.

The focus of the Productivity Conversation is to make sure those we mentor are going the right way and will get where they want to go. We want to help them experience meaningful results for their efforts; we know that consistent productivity moves us closer and closer to Uncommon Success.

What Is Productivity?

A classic definition of productivity that you might find in a business book would describe it as "the quality, state, or fact of being able to generate, create, enhance, or bring forth goods and services." Productivity is a clear accomplishment of the intended outcome. You can describe it as the ability to get the right stuff done, and get it done in an effective way. It is about getting intentional results.

Think of productivity in terms of shooting an arrow. Most people will practice their archery by setting up a target. They will step back and aim at the target, then release their arrow with the intent of hitting the target. "Intentional" is a key word here. We are talking about intentional results, not random results. Productivity is like hitting the target you set in advance. Lack of productivity would miss the mark. In my experience, I have missed the target on more than one occasion. What we want to avoid is becoming the type of people who shoot the arrow and then draw a circle around where the arrow lands, declaring success.

There are numerous challenges to consistently getting productive results. You may have a lack of clarity about which target is right for you. You may not even know where the target is and may lack focus. You may know where you are aiming but you are overcommitted. Everything becomes blurry when you juggle too many commitments and things fall.

Another mistake people make is misunderstanding the difference between *efficient* and *effective*. You can be very efficient in placing your ladder against a wall. But it isn't effective if it is leaning against the wrong wall. It is important to make sure you are effective in your efforts.

CHAPTER 7: HOW DO THEY KNOW WHERE WE ARE GOING?

The biggest challenge most likely comes from villainous enemies of productivity. I picture them hanging out together like a leather clad motorcycle gang. On the back of their black jackets are the words "Masters of Distraction."

Masters of Distraction

The leader of the Masters of Distraction gang is Bumper Car Karl. Karl is a master of business. Think of going on a bumper car ride at the county fair. Notice everyone is getting in their car. The power is turned on and the collisions begin. There is laughing and shouting. People are targeting specific cars. Some are the targets. Overall, it is a lot of fun. Eventually, the power is turned off, and everyone gets out of their car and the ride is over.

Bumper Car Karl does the same thing to us in life. He gets us into a bumper car named Busy. He helps us have fun. Maybe we are focused. We may even have some targets. But when we are finished, we haven't gone anywhere. Karl gets us so busy with the activities of the day that we never get around to building a road to go somewhere.

A teacher I heard using this illustration said that we could be building railroad tracks so we can fill a train with people who want to travel to an intended destination. Building tracks, driving a train to the destination, that is productivity. Karl doesn't like that.

Teddy Tech is another member of the gang. He likes to distract people with technology. He is especially good with cell phones, and he lures people with all kinds of apps. Whatever your preferred distraction, he has an app for that. Some people like to get busy using his apps of news sites, shopping, games and even productivity. He has a patch on his jacket proclaiming he was able to link the email to the phone. Now, most people feel lost without having their phone. What started out as a communication tool has transformed people, so they are often looking at their phone, rather than other people and the beauty surrounding them.

Teddy's girlfriend is Sally Social. She has been very creative in creating distractions. She partnered with Teddy and came up with Facebook, Twitter, Instagram, Pinterest and LinkedIn to name a few. She recently added a patch to her jacket for TikTok and Reels. She says this is just the beginning.

There are quite a few members in the gang, but I need to tell you about one more. He goes by the initials FOMO. Some say FOMO stands for "Fear of Missing Out." He has been able to use the tools created by others and combine them with current events. He can use weather, health, politics, war, economy, Netflix, Amazon and People Magazine. His list seems almost limitless. You name it and he can leverage it to become a major distraction.

You do not need to fear this gang. You can avoid them when you see them coming. The best way to avoid the Masters of Distraction is to be busy creating your Path to Productivity.

The Path to Productivity

There is a path that measures our readiness for productivity. You can follow it like a recipe in a cookbook or view it like a math equation: Plan x Skill x Fire = Readiness for Productivity. Each of these components will be broken down and explained in more detail below. Right now, I want to show you the power of the formula, helping you see its importance. Once you have your

Plan ready, you can give it a measurement on a scale of 1 to 10 (1 is low, 10 is high). You will do the same for Skill and Fire.

For example, let's imagine that my Plan is pretty well designed so I can give it an 8, and my Skill is a 5 but my Fire is a 2. The Readiness for Productivity score would by 8 x 5 x 2 = 80. Now, let's imagine my Plan is a 10, my Skill is a 10 but my heart is not in it, so my Fire is 0. The formula results would look like 10 x 10 x 0 = 0. Notice that I have to invest in all three elements; otherwise, I am not ready to be productive.

I was recently working with a client, and I walked them through the Readiness formula. When I asked how ready they were to get started on being more productive, the person replied, "I'm pretty ready." This person's scores were 5 x 7 x 4 = 140. When I pointed out that the highest possible score was 1000, they realized they had more work to do with their plan and the fire they were bringing to being productive. There is more to come with our Path to Productivity. Let's break down each of these elements into smaller pieces.

The Plan

The Plan has five keys to be effective. They are Destination (vision), Goals (targets), Strategy (map), Metrics (photos) and Accountability (integrity check).

1. Destination. We have covered the vision in the previous chapter. Right now, think of your vision as a destination. In order to be able to measure our effectiveness in fulfill-

ing the plan, we need to know where we are going. If I was living in California and headed to Washington State for a summer vacation, I would need to know where in Washington I am going. If I only decided that I needed to make it to Washington, I could pull the car over to the side of the road, once I drove through Portland and crossed the Columbia River. But then I would miss Mt. Rainier, Olympic National Park, the Space Needle and countless other possibilities. The more clearly you can describe your destination, the better your chance of arriving where you want to go.

2. Goals. Goals are targets we are aiming for along the way. A good plan will need some clear goals that you can you use to keep track of your progress. Start with your vision as your first and highest goal. Remember your list of everything you wanted to see, be, do and have? Pull out those lists and begin to determine the time frame for each item. Is it a one-, three-, or five-year goal? Your time frame might be different. That is okay! The important thing is to think through how long you think they might take to be reached.

Next, with a focus on productivity, circle the items on your list that will move you toward fulfilling your destination goal/vision. With circled goals, use the SMART system to shape and prioritize them. SMART is an acronym for Specific, Measurable, Actionable, Relevant and Time Bound. For example, if you have a goal to "be healthier," that is far too general and can be forgotten. To make it SMART you might say I want to lose twenty-five pounds by June 1st. That is Specific and Measurable (twenty-five pounds) and Time Bound (June 1st). Relevant to being healthier and something where you can take Action.

The final point on goals is to make sure they are written down. I do not know why this works. Some say it activates something in the brain that causes you to zero in on your goals, even subconsciously. What I do know is that, when you write down your goals, you are much more likely to accomplish them.

I was once challenged to write down ten goals, and I did. Then I forgot about the paper. A year later, the paper showed up and nine out of the ten goals had been accomplished.

There is something powerful at work when you write down your goals, and once you have a list, you are ready to begin putting together a strategy.

3. Strategy. Your strategy is like looking at a map and determining your desired route to arrive at your destination. You can use your circled goals that move you toward your destination and determine which ones are the best for the journey.

The Auxano organization has a great tool called the Vision Frame, which is used for organizational consulting. I often use it to teach clients how to think strategically about accomplishing their vision. It is a 1-4-1-4 model.

The top line is your vision or destination. This is your long-term goal or the fulfillment of your vision. It may take years to accomplish your vision, and only you can determine that. For the demonstration, I put in a three-to-seven-year time frame. But you can change that to meet your needs.

1-4-1-4 Strategy Plan

Vision/Destination 3-7 years
4 2-4 Year Goals
1 Year Goal
4 90 Day Goals

The next line down has four boxes, and these are goals that, when accomplished, will move you toward the fulfillment of your vision. They are building blocks that you may have discovered when you made your list of goals. They are important but they are not the final destination. They simply move you in the right direction.

CHAPTER 7: HOW DO THEY KNOW WHERE WE ARE GOING?

These top two lines can feel like you are just dreaming, and in some ways you are. You are visualizing future outcomes. What comes next is where the real power begins to reveal itself.

The next line down is a one-year goal. Choose this carefully, because it will be the launching pad for the journey to your vision. What is the one thing that, when you accomplish it, will be a clear victory? For example, I have a vision of where I am going with my life. But my one-year goal has been to get this book written and published. Getting the book into your hands is important because it helps move me forward for my visionary goals. After all, I still have the rest of my life.

The bottom line of our 1-4-1-4 box is for ninety-day goals. These are goals that can be knocked out within a three-month time frame. As you accomplish each of those goals, you can then replace them with new ninety-day goals. In that way, you can finish no less than sixteen goals that will help you fulfill your one-year goal. Working with a mentor, you can identify and clarify your strategy for best results.

4. Metrics. Think of metrics like you would think of photos you take while you are on a journey. You take a look at the photo, and it is a moment in time; it is not the whole story, but it shows you what is going on at the moment it was taken. Metrics are proof that you are on the path you decided to take. Because you have made your goals SMART, each one is time stamped and detailed. Another

trick is to make sure you are taking pictures of the right things.

I worked in and with churches for years. The metrics most churches were using to determine success were counting attendance and offerings. But those snapshots will only tell part of the story. I always thought it was better to count how many leaders they were developing through the ministry. How many small group leaders did they have? How many volunteers were contributing their time each week? Those two metrics would be a better indicator of the health of the church than nickels and noses.

5. Accountability. Who do you trust to tell you the truth? Once you have your plan in place, it is helpful to be accountable to someone. It could be an individual or a group. However, the sticking point is that we are usually hesitant to be evaluated by an outside party. But for the effectiveness of the plan, you want accountability. What gets inspected accomplishes what you expect.

That is your five-step planning phase for our Preparation for Productivity. Let's continue with looking at the skills for productivity.

Skills

Skills needed for success vary from project to project. You may need technical/technology skills, need legal, political or physical skills. There are many skills that may be necessary for ultimate success on your personal journey. I will only focus on three skills that are needed in any endeavor: Attitude, Emotional Quotient, and Communications. These are foundational and can be developed. They each have a significant influence on your productivity.

1. Attitude. The first skill zeros in on you. How do you manage yourself? How is your attitude? The good news is that, if you don't like your attitude, you can change it. Zig Ziglar taught that attitude is not only a choice but a skill to be learned. Dr. Martin E.P. Seligman from the University of Pennsylvania wrote an entire book dedicated to that premise. In *Learned Optimism*, he provides evidence that we can overcome negative thoughts and learn to control our attitude.

   The one practice that has helped me more than any other takes us back to the formula, E+R=O, which we discussed earlier. The knowledge that I didn't need to be a victim but could adjust outcomes by adjusting my response, empowered me. When I encountered upsetting events, I remember learning to repeat over and over the questions, "What can I control? What can I not control?" I learned to let go of trying to control what was impossible to control and worked on controlling myself. I no longer felt any need to rage against the world. I could slow down, take a breath and find a better response. That led to a much more peaceful and positive attitude.

2. Emotional Quotient. The second skill is your ability to interact with other people. This concept, which is shortened to EQ (Emotional Quotient), has grown in recent years and was popularized through the writing of Dan Goleman. EQ is classically defined as is the ability to manage both your own emotions and understand the emotions of people around you. It also is a skill that can be developed. The Mental Health American Association that focuses on workplace mental health suggests you can improve your EQ skills with some thoughtfulness and practice:

- Slow down your reactions to emotions. Next time you feel angry, try to sit with it before lashing out. Why are you angry? Did someone upset you? What do you think was the emotion underneath their behavior?
- Think about your strengths and weaknesses. No one is good at everything and that's okay! Know yourself and when to ask for—or offer—help.
- Make the effort to understand what people are communicating non-verbally. If you ask someone to help you on a project and they agree, but sound hesitant, recognize that they may feel overwhelmed or confused or they come from a different background and understanding than your own. It's important to validate and address that before moving forward.

- Work on communicating effectively and openly. Make sure your main point is clear. Cut out information that isn't relevant to the person you're talking with and give your full attention when someone else is speaking.

3. Communications. Our third skill for maximizing effective productivity is how we connect with others through our communications. The most important rule of communication is to make it clear and understandable. Do not try to impress people with your mastery of a great vocabulary. At least don't try to impress them with words they may not understand. Your goal is to make your thoughts as clear as possible and transfer them to others.

A skill to develop within communications is to understand "meaning." By that, I mean that people express a particular meaning when they communicate. You have a meaning that you are trying to get into others. The goal is to get the others to know what you "mean" or what you are talking about. If they know what you mean, you have communicated. Without the transfer of "meaning", you have not communicated.

We can all work at improving our communication skills, whether it be vocal, through writing or even body language. Dr. Albert Mehrabian's 7-38-55 Communication model says that 7 percent of the transfer of meaning, feelings and attitudes takes place through the words we use in spoken communications. Tone and voice account for 38 percent of the messaging. The remaining 55 percent of communication takes place through the body language we use.⁶ This is why our next category of preparedness for productivity is important. The fire we bring to our communication has far more to do with our effectiveness than words alone.

Fire

The third piece of our (P x S x F) formula is the fire. When I am talking about fire, I'm looking at passion, focus, and determination.

Passion. The Bible talks about doing things with all your heart. "Whatever you do, work at it with all your heart" (Colossians 3:23, NIV). That is passion.

In their book, *The Passion Test*, Janet and Chris Atwood describe passion this way: "Passion is the inner fire that propels you forward through a combination of love for what you're doing and the inner sense of purpose that comes connecting to one's deepest passions."

The question becomes how strong is your passion for this journey? To ensure your passion, you want to make sure you love your vision.

Focus. How much focus you can bring to your efforts for productivity will determine the pace at which you can move. Are you able to concentrate on your project, or do you have too many distractions? Steve Jobs said, "Focusing is about saying, 'No'." Learning to say No to the distractions is a powerful tool in your arsenal. Every time you say No, you are freeing yourself to say yes and give time to the right things.

CHAPTER 7: HOW DO THEY KNOW WHERE WE ARE GOING?

Determination. The ability to carry on when the going gets tough is another piece of living with fire. You could call this commitment, resolve, dedication, will power, persistence or grit. Whatever word you choose, it is that internal drive that just won't let you quit.

With these major pieces in place, you have the make-up for effective productivity. There is one more piece to the formula that must be looked at. If we don't, the entire structure will fail to produce any results.

The Final Piece of the Formula — Action

The final piece is to energize or take Action. Remember, our formula is like a math problem: Plan x Skills x Fire. We give each piece a score on a scale of 1 to 10. Next, we need to place all three pieces inside the parenthesis (PxSxF). This will give us one number. Then we add the final component of Action to the formula.

Our final formula is complete with: (P x S x F) x A = Productivity.

This next point is vitally important, and if you get it, it will change your life. The "Action" component is not on a scale of 1 – 10. Rather it is either zero or 10.

This entire chapter on Productivity is based on getting things done. Think of the TV show *Star Trek* for a moment. As a kid (maybe even now) I loved the transporter device that moved Captain Kirk and the crew from the Enterprise mothership to the surface of the planet, or wherever they wanted to go. However, no one was going anywhere until the right words were said. It only happened when someone commanded the engineer to "Energize."

Think of your productivity formula like that. You can have a fantastic plan. Rate it a 10.

You have tremendous and refined skills. Rate your skill level a 10. You can bring the fire and be very excited about your future. Rate your fire at a 10. If you multiply (10 x 10 x 10) that equals 1000. If, however you don't energize, taking action on a plan, your productivity drops to zero. You cannot be productive without action. But with energizing productivity, we move closer and closer to Uncommon Success. Follow this formula and you will definitely be worth knowing.

If you mentor someone through these first four conversations, they will grow in character and productivity. They will experience change and disruption of their old patterns

In the next chapter, we will go to the final conversation and answer this question: How do we stay authentic in the midst of the soul-shaking that comes from rapid deep change?

CHAPTER 7: HOW DO THEY KNOW WHERE WE ARE GOING?

Questions for Reflection

1. Looking back, when have you been most productive?

2. How do you feel about a results orientation versus a busy orientation?

3. Describe a plan you are currently working on.

The Authenticity Conversation: Who Am I Now?

"It may be hard for an egg to turn into a bird: it would be a jolly sight harder for it to learn to fly while remaining an egg. We are like eggs at present. And you cannot go on indefinitely being just an ordinary, decent egg. We must be hatched or go bad."
— C. S. Lewis

Surprise and Change

Surprises are not always welcome. In my family, we didn't have a great track record when it came to celebrating birthdays. But this year it was going to be different. The drive was uneventful. My wife didn't ask any questions while we traveled and walked in the door to our son's home. The plan had worked. Everyone successfully arrived early, hiding their cars outside and themselves inside. As we came through the door, the small crowd shouted, "Surprise! Happy Birthday!" It really was a big surprise for my wife. The rest of us had conspired to celebrate her birthday in a way which we usually don't. And yes, she was surprised. It was only afterward that I was informed how much she dislikes surprises. She didn't feel prepared and was uncomfortable being the center of attention. I kind of knew that, but I went ahead with the plan anyway.

There is more to the story, but the point is that not every surprise is all that great. Especially if they make you feel ill prepared and uncomfortable.

There are good surprises, and when they arrive, we should celebrate. When an unexpected refund shows up in the mail or we receive a generous gift. He asks the big question, and she says, "Yes." Those are wonderful moments.

However, some people don't like surprises because they can come wrapped in sadness, loss or disappointment. It could be a health crisis, the death of a friend, a financial setback or a family member who disappoints you. When you think about it, most surprises aren't viewed favorably. The biggest surprise for me on my journey was that, after some success and change, I ended up asking the question, "Who Am I Now?"

CHAPTER 8: THE AUTHENTICITY CONVERSATION: WHO AM I NOW?

If surprises are often looked upon unfavorably, change is even more challenging. People don't like change, but they do want things to be better. However, most of us would prefer not going through change to arrive at the "better."

Here is the issue. We have already talked about the importance of personal and unique identity, but now we are moving into a deeper level of understanding regarding identity. When you follow this strategic path, your life will change. And when this change occurs, it often leads to a surprise. The big surprise is that you may not feel like you are comfortable in your own skin. When you go through this process and begin to experience deep change, it will lead to, "Who am I now?" The question may come several times as you experience different breakthroughs.

The arrival of this sudden question is evidence that the journey is working. You are not who you used to be. Your integrity has grown by being honest with yourself about where you truly are in your life. Your unique identity journey has given you more clarity about who you are and what makes you special in this world. This has given you the personal freedom to craft a compelling vision for your life. With that clear vision, you have been able to develop and execute on a plan that is motivating and productive. You have clear goals, but they are not what they used to be. You have done all that work. Now you may be thinking, *how is it possible that I am uncomfortable and feeling ill prepared?*

It is like going on a successful diet and your clothes no longer fit. You are leaner and healthier. But with a strategic journey to Uncommon Success, the change isn't in the clothes; it is the change of becoming comfortable in your own skin. When we can accomplish that, we can risk being authentic. But the journey is not without barriers.

The Enemies of Authenticity

Enemy 1 – The Wall

The Wall is another way of saying you are stuck. When you don't feel comfortable with who you are, after you have changed, that is the feeling of being stuck. When reading books focused on human and personal development, you will notice language about getting stuck. Terry Walling's book titled, *Stuck – Navigating the Transitions of Life and Leadership* uses the seminal work of Dr. J. Robert Clinton. Walling provides guidance on getting unstuck from a number of life transition barriers.

In their book, *The Critical Journey*, Janet Hagberg and Robert A. Guelich talk about 6 stages of personal growth in a spiritual journey that eventually leads to stage 6, a Life of Love. The most interesting part of the book for me was stage 4, where they spend time talking about The Wall. "The Wall represents a place where another layer of transformation occurs, and a renewed life of faith begins for those who feel called and have the courage to move into it." In another passage they write, "Not everyone goes through the Wall. Some stop or get stuck at earlier stages in the journey and never get to the Wall. Others decide at the Wall to return to an earlier stage. Still others get stuck in front of the Wall…"[7]

The goal when facing the Wall is to get through it. It is not possible to go around, dig under or fly over it. Like the prelude to a *Mission Impossible* movie, "Your assignment, should you choose to accept it" is to go through the Wall.

CHAPTER 8: THE AUTHENTICITY CONVERSATION: WHO AM I NOW?

Enemy 2 – Impostor Syndrome and the Fear of Not Being Enough

The Impostor Syndrome is a mental condition in which an effective, successful person feels like a fraud. Even if the person has reached a certain high level of accomplishment, they are afraid people will find out they really don't have the necessary skills, knowledge or talents for the work and will be seen as a phony. The irony is this seems to hit those who have been successful. I named Impostor Syndrome "Foster." While not everyone suffers from Foster the Impostor, research shows that up to 70 percent of people do. We must listen to that voice in our head saying, "What if they find out who I really am?" or "Who do you think you are?" Foster the Impostor is so common that he is clearly number 1 in making us feel uncomfortable in our own skin.

The Impostor Syndrome reminds me of the line from Walt Kelly's, pogo comic strip of years ago: "We have met the enemy and he is us."

It is true that Impostor Syndrome can take different forms. You might recognize yourself in one of these types.

1. The Perfectionist. This person gets caught up with the idea that they could have done better. They find it hard to celebrate because no matter how well they performed, they focus on what wasn't perfect. Foster the Impostor might say, "You're not good enough."

2. The Expert. Experts find value in how much they know. The problem lies in the fact that there is always something you don't know. The voice might be heard saying, "You don't know enough."

3. The Genius. The Genius is the person who has had things come easily to them. They were the ones who got good grades, maybe even straight As. They tend to set a high bar for their expectations. The problem for the Genius is when things don't come easily, when they don't get things right on the first try. If it takes a longer time to learn something new, the voice in their head might say, "You are not smart enough."

4. The Soloist. The Soloist is the person who is afraid to ask for help. They don't ask because they are afraid that asking others for help will cause others to think they are phony. The thought is that if I can solve this on my own that will prove my worth. The voice in their head says, "Prove to them that you don't need any help. Otherwise, they will know you aren't good enough."

5. The Superhero. The Superhero is convinced that they are matched up with people who are superior in abilities and thus feel inferior. They will work harder and longer to measure up and cover their sense of inadequacy. The Superhero can get caught up in a double bind of thinking: "I can't measure up, but I have to. I have to work harder, but I can't be good enough."

You will notice that I made sure the little voice was always including the word "enough." In the final analysis, feeling like an impostor is always centered around believing you are not "enough" of something. It could be good enough, smart enough, fast enough, kind enough or simply not enough. It is very difficult to feel authentic if the voice in your head continues to whisper these debilitating thoughts. When we listen, we can get frozen, and it only magnifies that annoying voice.

Just in case you are wondering, there is another possible voice. There is an opposite to Impostor Syndrome called the Dunning-Kruger effect.[8] It occurs when people overestimate their abilities. If you have ever watched the movie *Napoleon Dynamite*, you will see this behavior in the character Uncle Rico. Uncle Rico loves to throw the football, claiming he could throw the ball over the mountains. He also carries bitterness, because he believes that his high school team would have been champions if the coach had just put him in to play.

You may be thinking at this point, *what am I supposed to do to be the most authentic person I long to be?* Below, you'll find three major concepts to help break through your personal Walls and overcome impostor syndrome.

Deep Change and the Journey to Authenticity

Earlier in the book, I talked about deep change. Change happens in our lives during the first four conversations. But deep change, becoming more authentic, occurs when we practice three critical mindset changes. This is for the courageous.

Author Robert Quinn points out that, "Each of us has the potential to change the world. Because the price of change is so high, we seldom take on the challenge. Our fears blind us to the possibilities of excellence."[9]

What these mindset changes have in common is that they all require a type of faith. For many, there will be new beliefs about how life works. But if you can wrap your mind around these concepts, the payoff is a life of growing authenticity moving us toward Uncommon Success.

1. The Critical Mindset – Self-Acceptance

The first critical mindset is to understand the power of self-acceptance. Earlier, we talked about the importance of self-esteem. Self-esteem is a powerful weapon in transforming our lives. It is important that we see ourselves as lovable and capable.

I once taught a seminar that was designed around the work of rational emotive behavioral therapy, or REBT for short. In that seminar, we learned about the value of self-esteem but also of its shortcomings. In this approach, self-esteem is defined as the attempt to measure your value as a person or your self-worth.

There are two components of self-esteem:

A. What you think other people think about you ... or how much you think these other people care about you.

B. What you think of the behaviors or traits you "do."
   - Traits would be things such as being courageous, orderly and punctual.
   - Behaviors are more specific like swimming well or how you barbeque a steak.

You can begin to see the issue when you believe your self-esteem is developed around what others think of you. Sometimes someone will think highly of you. Other times, someone close to you may be upset with you. The danger is that if we measure our self-esteem based on what others think, or what we think they think in that given moment, our self-esteem can rise or fall. Add to that the issue of behaviors and traits. Sometimes we do things well. Sometimes we don't.

If you are at the lake and can't swim as well as others, how might that affect your self-esteem?

CHAPTER 8: THE AUTHENTICITY CONVERSATION: WHO AM I NOW?

Another issue we taught in the seminar is that it is possible for some to only focus on one person's view of you and get tunnel vision. The problem with tunnel vision is that you may have wonderful relationships with 99 percent of the people in your life. But a focus on the 1 percent where the relationships aren't great can cause your self-esteem to drop. For example, if you compare your swimming to an Olympic champion, you will never measure up.

Another trap is dichotomous thinking. This means things are either fully one way or the other. It is seen in the person who, after making a mistake, declares that they are 100 percent worthless. Or worse, if another person makes a mistake, they are 100 percent terrible. It is all or nothing for the dichotomous thinker.

The assumption of self-esteem is that it is possible to rate, measure or evaluate yourself and assign a value level. But to do so, you would need to know your present behavior, past behavior, conscious motivations, unconscious motivations, the consequences to others and to self. You would also need to know how much other people care and think about you.

In the seminar, we would provide this definition of the "self." We would say, "You are the sum total of all the experiences, both internal and external, that you have encountered during your entire lifetime."

It is estimated by some researchers that we each have one billion experiences for every twenty years of life. On average, with great motivation, we may be able to access up to 40 percent of our total experiences. Of that 40 percent, the average person can recall about 1 percent.

The big question then becomes, "Knowing what you know and what is required that you know, is it really possible to rate yourself on an arbitrary scale? The answer is "No!" You are too complex to know all of you. If that is true, you as a person cannot ever be truly rated.

The solution to this issue is to give yourself a great gift—the gift of Self-Acceptance. No one else can give it to you. Only you have the power to give yourself this gift.

Even with my background as a clergyman, I have tried not to make this an overtly religious book. But when it comes to the deep work of becoming authentic, there are a lot of faith principles at work. This giving yourself the gift of self-acceptance is an act of faith. It is like divine grace. In the Christian tradition, divine grace is a gift from the Heavenly Father, and it cannot be earned. It comes to us through our faith.

Self-acceptance is acceptance of myself based on nothing more than realizing my only choices are to accept myself or not accept myself. If we do accept ourselves with our faults, flaws and flubs, it changes how we view the world and our place in it. Here is an illustration.

The play "Man of LaMancha" centers on a bumbling and confused Alonso Quijano. He is an old gentleman who has read so many books of chivalry and thought so much about injustice that he has lost his mind and sets out as a knight-errant. Quijano renames himself, Don Quixote de La Mancha, and goes off to find adventures with his Squire, Sancho Panza. On their journey, Don Quixote meets a bar maid and part time prostitute named Aldonza. When he sees her in the Inn, he claims that she is his lady Dulcinea, to whom he has sworn eternal loyalty. While she is annoyed with his obvious misunderstanding, she allows him to continue to call her by the new name.

At the conclusion of the play, Don Quixote is dying, and Aldonza/Dulcinea comes to visit him. After he has died, Sancho is grieving his friend's death. Aldonza tries to comfort him, saying that Alonso Quijano may be dead, but Don Quixote lives on. In one of the most profound moments in the play, Sancho addresses her as Aldonza, and she replies, "My name is Dulcinea." In that one moment she has given herself the gift of new self-acceptance. She can no longer view herself as the prostitute Aldonza. She has become a new person. That is what self-acceptance does. It changes your world from the inside out. You will begin to live in a way, free from the declarations of others. It is the declaration that you own for yourself that matters.

2. *The Transitions Mindset*

The next step into deep change as we progress on our journey to authenticity is developing a Transitions Mindset. *Transitions* is the key word, because we are distinguishing it from the word change. To define the difference, change is an event. Transition is a process. People will often say that they do not like change. What they usually mean is they don't like the process of transition that is required when change occurs. Let me say it again—change is an event. It is something that simply happens. Transition is a process of figuring out how you will manage the change that has impacted your life.

Not all change is bad. When you get married, you enter into a changed relationship. It was a choice going in. When you said "I do", your life changed. You now live together. You plan together. You prepare meals and manage your budget together. But the change isn't where the work in marriage takes place. It is the process of transitioning your beliefs and practices. You live together but how do you decide where your socks go? You can eat together but who establishes the menu and buys the groceries? You can celebrate the holidays together but what traditions will you follow? These are transition questions.

Let's talk about you and the change that has happened inside of you on your strategic journey to Uncommon Success. You feel like a different person, and you may think, *How can I be authentic when I am not sure about who I am now?*

The answer does not lie in trying to figure out what has changed. The answer lies in using a transitions mindset. A transition mindset does not focus on change but rather the sense of discomfort. Ask yourself, *where is this discomfort coming from? Why am I feeling uncomfortable?* And the most important questions you can ask are:

- What am I holding onto?
- What is so dear to me that I don't want to let go?
- What do I need to let go of?
- Why is it so important to me that I allow it to control me?
- What do I need to bring to a conclusion?
- What is in my life that I need to finish?
- What potentialities am I missing?
- How can this new reality be moved from toleration to celebration?

Then you can begin to look forward with anticipation questions.

With a transition mindset you are allowed to not pretend your life is all together. You are on a journey and free to recognize yourself as a work in progress. Then we are free to accept we are in transition.

When you hear the song "Glory Road" by Neil Diamond, you will notice that it has an interesting twist. When Mr. Diamond wrote the song in 1969, the final line was different than what he sings later in his career. The song is about a troubadour hitting the road looking for glory through his music. He travels the country singing and playing, and eventually others ask him how to find Glory Road.[9] In the original song, his final line is "Now I know Glory Road won't set me free."

In the Hot August Nights III concert, 2012, at the Los Angeles' Greek Theater, a celebration of the 40th anniversary of the first Hot August Nights concert, Diamond changed the last lyric. Instead of singing, "Now I know Glory Road won't set me free" he sang, "Now I know Glory Road is right here in me." That is a good example of a transition mindset. The troubadour had let go of looking for glory coming from outside of himself. He instead recognized that the glory he was after was inside himself all along.

If this topic interests you, I recommend Dr. William Bridges' book *Transitions – Making Sense of Life's Changes*.[10] He dives deeply into the full range of issues around transition and offers sound advice for anyone who struggles with the process.

3. Fear-Courage-Action Mindset

When we think about being comfortable in our own skin, we have to recognize that part of the discomfort is simply based in fear. This is new territory; we have never been here before. We may be afraid of what people will think of us. We may fear the consequences that will come with more success. Or we may simply be nervous about breaking through our previous barriers. To tackle fear with action is the last part of our work of becoming authentic.

Our third mindset is the Fear-Courage-Action Mindset. This may sound like the simplest form of advice but feel the fear ... and do it anyway. Susan Jeffers wrote a book with that exact title in 1987 and it has sold over 2 million copies.

This mindset is about three things: the acknowledgement of our fear, building up courage and taking action. There is nothing more authentic than admitting when you are afraid. There is nothing more powerful than brushing the fear aside and taking action.

For years I wanted to be a speaker. I had done some public speaking, but it was not my primary responsibility. In 1998, I had the opportunity to go to a weeklong seminar that concluded with a challenge to break through my barriers. The challenge was to stand up and allow another person to hold the point of an arrow on my throat. My task was to thrust myself forward. This was to create tension on the shaft to the degree that the shaft would snap before the point penetrated my throat. Let me point out that the arrows were real. At first, I didn't believe them.

Different speakers have different techniques to help you see you are capable of doing things you didn't think you could, like Tony Robbins and his famous fire walk. At the moment they were demonstrating how this arrow challenge would work, I was thinking that a fire walk would be preferable. Even though the demonstration was successful, I still wasn't convinced. People lined up to have the arrow placed on their throat. I watched one person after another thrust themselves forward and arrow after arrow snapped. I was still not convinced. The line was getting shorter and shorter, and I was still letting others go in front of me. The time came when there were only two of us left. The lady in front of me was in her 70s, and I watched as the fragile senior citizen thrust herself forward.

I should add, as people thrust forward, they also would yell what they wanted for a breakthrough in their life. My time had

CHAPTER 8: THE AUTHENTICITY CONVERSATION: WHO AM I NOW?

come. No one was behind me, and I was the last and least courageous. The man picked up an arrow and placed it on my throat. I somehow summoned my courage and thrust forward yelling, "I want to be a public speaker!" The arrow broke. No medical attention was sought. Instead, I left there knowing that I could become a public speaker. Well, at least I knew that I had enough courage to try. After spending years on the road speaking all over the U.S. and having had the opportunity to speak in the U.K., I continued to work at my skills as a public speaker.

As we close out this chapter, understand that you have the capacity to experience deep change and be comfortable in your own skin.

Mastering the mindset skills of Self-Acceptance, Transition and Fear/Courage/Action leads to an integrated holistic life moving us closer and closer to Uncommon Success.

Now that we have covered *the 5 Conversations*, in the next chapter, we will look at two key results of Uncommon Success.

Questions for Reflection

1. Can you describe a moment when you realized you had changed in some way?

2. Is imposter syndrome something you have experienced? How did you manage those feelings?

3. On a scale of 1 to 10 (low to high), how would you rate your self-esteem? Self-acceptance? How would you describe the difference between the two?

Light A Fire — Choices, Leadership and Legacy

> "Life is a matter of choices, and every
> choice you make makes you."
> — John C Maxwell

Bad Choices

My earliest ideas for writing a book were centered on the lessons in life I have learned the hard way. My working title was always *Don't Do This – Daily Doses of Delayed Intelligence*. My primary reason focused on a bad experience early in life.

It impacted not only my own life but others in my family. I made a series of bad choices.

In the summer of 1960, our family was enjoying the annual visit to my uncle's farm in western Washington. It was a place of enormous fun for town kids. That is what we were—town kids.

My Uncle Bill had acres of pastureland with cows and cow pies. Of course, they were a great source of entertainment. The farm was bordered on the north and east side with northwest forest and typical, heavy underbrush, where the deer and rabbits would emerge. I found the wildlife mysterious. There were also chickens running around, pecking away at the ground. Best of all, there was a big barn fifty yards north of the house. It contained stalls for the cows, bales and bales of stored hay and an upper loft filled with loose straw. Oh, how I remember smell of the barn! Come to think of it, there was an outhouse too. That was a new experience. We loved going to Uncle Bill's farm. There were so many things to do, which may make the next part of this story sound a little off.

Being six years old, you would think I would have better things to do. But I was several years younger than my siblings, and there were no other kids my age around. Even on the farm, a six-year-old left on his own can get bored.

One day, I went into the kitchen and snatched a matchbook when no one was looking. I have no real understanding of my motivations at the time. As I have told the story over the years, I have made up the excuse that I had a scientific mind and wondered if certain things would burn.

My first experiment was done in secret. I took a comic book with me to the barn and climbed up into the straw in the loft. If anyone had seen me headed that way alone, they would have thought I was going to read my comic book. Unfortunately, I

CHAPTER 9: LIGHT A FIRE – CHOICES, LEADERSHIP AND LEGACY

couldn't read yet. Instead, I lit a match and then I lifted the comic up in the air about head height. I suppose the scientific question would be, "Do comic books burn?" The answer came quickly as the paper caught fire and burned upward to my hand.

I dropped the flaming pages into the straw. The straw caught fire. My life could have ended there, but I was able to stamp out the flames. My heart was racing. I covered the charred paper and straw with fresh straw and left the barn thinking ... well, I don't know what I was thinking. I can't say that I know, because I tried more experiments later.

That same day, I was upstairs alone, sent to bed early. My bedtime was far earlier than anyone else. And if you know anything about northern summers, there was still daylight. I wasn't ready to sleep, and I still had my matches.

My second experiment of the day was to light matches to see if I could make pennies melt. But it didn't matter how many matches I put on a penny, they never came close to melting. My third and final experiment came when I started wandering around upstairs looking for other possible items to melt. I discovered a pile of foam rubber pillows in the back of the house. Surely it would be interesting to watch a pillow melt. I lit the match, held it to the lowest pillow in the pile, and sadly it did not melt. The foam exploded into a flame that consumed the rest of the pillows in a flash and then the fire climbed the wall. It was the second time in one day that my life could have ended. There was no stamping out this fire.

I ran for the stairs, running down screaming, "Fire, Fire, Fire!" No one paid any attention to me.

My Auntie Ann finally stopped her card game and calmly said she would take care of it. She walked up the stairs with a pan of water. It was her turn to come running down with the same message, "Fire, Fire, Fire!"

I will pause the story there and give a summary of the results. My Uncle Bill's house burned to the ground. Everything burned. It was the first time I had ever seen my mother cry. We drove the 300 miles home, with only the clothes on our backs and where it became a forbidden subject to talk about.

There are a variety of lessons to learn from my story besides, "Don't let six-year-old boys play with matches." Most of them have to do with my life after the fire. These lessons provide the context for what I want you to understand as we finish this book about strategic mentoring.

People make choices. Some are good and some are bad. I believe strategic mentoring can help people move their lives forward, especially after bad decisions.

Words of Life

When I pointed out that the subject of my tragic childhood foolishness was a forbidden topic in our home, that experience was not without impact on me. It drove home the point that what I did was unspeakably bad. Unknowingly, my parent's decision to not talk about it caused me to grow up with a deep, underlying sense of shame and guilt. Here is my point. I had no one to talk to.

Thirty-four years after the fire, Uncle Bill attended an event where I was being recognized. He surprised me because I didn't know he had arranged to attend. As an adult, I had very rarely seen him. He was 87 years old and looked just the same. I walked up to thank him for coming, and then I heard myself saying something about the fire all those years before. I asked if

CHAPTER 9: LIGHT A FIRE – CHOICES, LEADERSHIP AND LEGACY

he remembered it, and he laughed, saying he did. Then I pointed out that we had never talked about it and would he please forgive me. His response was life changing.

He laughed and looked at me with his head tilted to one side and asked, "Didn't they tell you?"

Now I was confused. He repeated his question, "Didn't they tell you?"

I asked him, "What do you mean?"

He asked again, "Didn't they tell you about what happened after the fire?" He went on, laughing as he spoke. "That old farmhouse was a dried-up rat trap, but I had insurance. I got a new house out of it. It was one of the best things that ever happened for me."

Up until that moment, I had lived 85 percent of my lifetime under guilt and shame for what I had done, while he had lived with a completely different perspective of joy and gladness. In that short exchange, he gave me the words of life.

Mentors are in a unique position to have that same opportunity for giving words of life. I'm not saying that every mentoring relationship will uncover deep wounds from decades before. But I am saying that an outside voice can give words of life when they look at things from a different perspective.

One more point from this story. Later, I realized I endured that sense of shame and guilt unnecessarily. I cannot help but wonder how many people are struggling unnecessarily with issues in their lives. If they had a trusted, caring, listening mentor, their lives could potentially be changed dramatically. I am convinced that, if we had more people who are prepared to be strategic mentors engaging in life-giving conversations, over time we can make the world a better place. It does sound like a cliché, but I think we can change the world one conversation at a time.

Leadership

As we come to the end of studying the strategic mentoring path for Uncommon Success, you now realize that this journey is one of personal development. You also can see that it is a path that can be traveled multiple times over the course of your life. Once you have learned the strategic path, you could use it as a guide annually to make the most out of the year.

If you continue to think about and lead others in these *5 Conversations*, another benefit will be a foundation for your leadership development. John C. Maxwell has long said that "Leadership is influence." There is a lot of truth to that brief definition. A person who knows where they are, who they are, where they are going and is getting there will always be a person with more influence. And when that same person grows through barrier after barrier, remaining comfortable in their own skin on the journey, their influence will be pronounced.

I like a different definition of leadership. I am not sure who said it first and I can't find an attribution. "Leadership is disruption." As a strategic mentor, you will have a positive path for creating needed disruption in a mentee's life, as well as your own.

My favorite understanding of leadership comes from Rabbi Edwin Friedman, who teaches that a healthy leader is self-differentiated. That means that a person understands who they are, and they know how to be comfortable in their own skin.

You can easily use this *5 Conversation* process for personal development and leadership development. In many ways, personal development is leadership development.

CHAPTER 9: LIGHT A FIRE – CHOICES, LEADERSHIP AND LEGACY

Legacy

What do you want to leave behind? And how do you want to be remembered after you are gone? These are the two key questions around legacy.

Pericles was a 5th century BC Greek politician and general, who was responsible for the building of the Acropolis, including the Parthenon in Athens. He obviously left a legacy of incredible construction. But he had this to say about legacy: "What you leave behind is not what is engraved in stone monuments, but what is woven into the lives of others."

I find it fascinating that a man so well-known was concerned about his legacy in the lives of others.

Back to choices. What legacy do you want to leave?

Personally, I have always appreciated the Native American parable of the two wolves.

An old Cherokee is teaching his grandson about life. "A fight is going on inside me," he said to the boy. "It is a terrible fight, and it is between two wolves. One is evil—he is anger, envy, sorrow, regret, greed, arrogance, self-pity, guilt, resentment, inferiority, lies, false pride, superiority, and ego." He continued, "The other is good—he is joy, peace, love, hope, serenity, humility, kindness, benevolence, empathy, generosity, truth, compassion, and faith. The same fight is going on inside you—and inside every other person, too."

The grandson thought about it for a minute and then asked his grandfather, "Which wolf will win?"

The old Cherokee simply replied, "The one you feed."

Legacy is about which wolf you want to feed.

So, what? What Choice Is Right for You?

Have you ever had an experience where you tell your story and the response you get from your friend is, "So what?" It can be discouraging or helpful.

I spent many years speaking in churches. One thing that was consistent was one of my wife's questions about my messages. Before I would speak, or sometimes after, she would ask me the question, "So What?" That's a good question.

As we come to the end of this book, I want to leave you with the same question. So, what?

So, what? There it is for you to wrestle. What will you do with this information? You have some key ingredients for engaging in substantive conversations. As I see it, you have three clear choices:

1. You can choose not to engage with the book and the journey. This could be one more book on your shelf, because it is not the right time for you. But you can probably think of someone you know who could use it.

2. You can choose to personally go on the *5 Conversation* journey. You can use the information and the process to help yourself move toward deep change and Uncommon Success.

3. You can choose to use *the 5 Conversations* process to mentor someone throughout the journey. You have the opportunity to guide another person, so they can experience deep change and Uncommon Success. You can help

them become a person who is more concerned with being worth knowing rather than well known.

Final Suggestions

If you choose to go on this journey for yourself or decide to become a strategic mentor, I commend you for wanting to get started. I do have some simple suggestions for you.

1. Find someone who can be a mentor to walk you through. They do not have to be an expert on *the 5 Conversations* but you can ask them to read the book and hold you accountable. That is the key word—accountability. Having someone to talk to is the point of this process. It is not the same experience if you seek to do it alone. To help you do this well, you can find a Mentor Checklist on the website www.stevenbwelling.com

2. When you find someone who agrees to serve as your mentor and you have both agreed to the guidelines, be consistent in having your targeted conversations. You will both be encouraged and challenged.

3. Be patient with yourself and the process of change. John C. Maxwell likes to say that, "People change when they … Hurt enough that they have to, Learn enough that they want to, and Receive enough that they are able to." It is possible that you are ready for change. But deep change comes with time and discomfort. This won't be physical discomfort. Instead, these pains will be in your

heart and soul as you search out who you really are and who you are intended to become.

4. If you choose to become a mentor for someone, be selective. You will be investing your time and attention to help them. You don't want a relationship where it feels like you're pushing a boulder uphill. Instead, you are looking for someone ready to invest their time and effort. You want to detect a bit of fire in the individual. Ask yourself, are they eager? Are they hungry? Are they willing and able to dedicate the energy?

   It is possible that your mentee is struggling with commitment, then you definitely have something to talk about. It may be that they are stuck or knocked down by one of the enemies. If that is the case, it will be a strategic time to help them make significant progress or guide them to new levels of understanding about themselves. These are the opportunities that make mentoring rewarding.

5. Serve your mentee. Strategic Mentoring (mentoring with a plan and a purpose) is built on servant-leadership. It will require a servant's heart that is dedicated to the success of your mentee. You will want to ask two questions consistently. What challenges are you facing right now? How can I serve you?

CHAPTER 9: LIGHT A FIRE – CHOICES, LEADERSHIP AND LEGACY

Final Thought

We have come to the end of this book, but we have not come to the end. This may be just the beginning for you. Maybe you feel like you are capable of being a deeper, noble person. Maybe you have more capacity as a self-aware leader. You have choices to consider as you think about your own legacy.

Let me take you back to the beginning. Being worth knowing is of more importance than being well known. That is Uncommon Success. With this book, you have the foundational tools to be a strategic mentor using *the 5 Conversations* pathway. It is possible others can experience deep change with your help. My hope is that you will consider becoming a strategic mentor to help others on that path. My greatest hope is that, one day, you will be able to say of being a mentor, "Didn't they tell you? It was the best thing that has ever happened to me."

Questions for Reflection

1. Can you describe a time in your life when it would have helped you to have a strategic mentor?

2. What is your definition of leadership?

3. Why do you think you might enjoy being a strategic mentor for someone?

Notes

1. Swindoll, C., 1999. Intimacy with the Almighty. Nashville, Tenn.: J. Countryman, p.13.

2. Quinn, R., 1996. Deep Change. New York: Jossey-Bass, p.3.

3. Wheatley, M., 2009. Turning To One Another. San Francisco: Berrett-Koehler Publishers. pp. 22-23, 27

4. https://en.wikipedia.org/wiki/Zelig

5. Canfield, J., 2015. The Success Principles. 2nd ed. New York: Morrow- Harper Collings, pp.6-7.

6. https://www.rightattitudes.com/2008/10/04/7-38-55-rule-personal-communication/

7. Hagberg, J. and Guelich, R., 1989. The Critical Journey. Salem: Sheffield Publishing Company, pp.114-115.

8. https://www.britannica.com/science/Dunning-Kruger-effect

9. Neil Diamond, Glory Road lyrics © Universal Tunes

10. Dr. William Bridges, Transitions – Making Sense of Life's Changes, De Capo Press, 2004

Acknowledgments

I would like to acknowledge all my mentors who have helped guide me through life. You may not know it, but you helped shape my life. I wish I could acknowledge everyone who poured into me and helped me learn from life's lessons. I do want to remember Loren Wenz, Larry Johnson, Dick Daniels, Keith LaGesse, John Lunsford, Gregg Nelson, Richard Sturm, Brian Ancell, Jan Hettinga, Joe Donaldson, Priscilla Saari, and David Bush. All were people who believed in me.

I want to express special appreciation to two people. First, I want to thank Jeremy Brown who patiently walked with me through the two-year process of creating this book. Without his continual personal encouragement, wisdom, and belief in me, I would not have completed this project.

Second, with deep gratitude, I acknowledge Patty Aubery. It was her mentoring over the past four years that made me aware that I had something to say. I remember the day when I asked her what she thought the next breakthrough goal should be for me. Without hesitation she said, "Write your book." Thank you, Patty, for investing in my life and helping me continue to break through my barriers. You truly are an extraordinary mentor!

Oct. 8, 2023

Dear Eddie,

    I was very blessed to meet Steve Welling last week as he came to town to speak at his childhood church Hillyard Baptist Church.

    He was a best friend and fellow paper boy with my late husband, Ed Dahlstrom.

    Ed Dahlstrom introduced Steve to his first Bible Camp. Ed separated from his many Christian friends when he chose drugs and alcohol over the peace found in Jesus.

    The were blessed to hear from me that Ed got sober and served the Lord in Spokane for many many years before he passed.

About the Author

Steven Welling was born and raised in Spokane, WA to hard-working parents. He graduated from Whitworth College in Spokane and then earned a Master of Divinity degree from Bethel Theological Seminary in St. Paul, MN. After 28 years in pastoral ministry and business, he became the Regional President of Converge Northwest, where he served for 13 years. Steve currently lives in the Pacific Northwest and serves leaders and organizations through his business, Strategic Mentor. He and his wife, Susie, have been blessed with three adult children and seven grandchildren and enjoy sharing good stories, reading, and traveling.

THE 5 CONVERSATIONS

About the Company

Strategic Mentor serves the needs of emerging and stuck leaders who want to experience uncommon success with their careers and life. One of our goals is to teach the process of strategic mentoring in churches and organizations in order to develop whole and healthy people who can experience uncommon success in life.